STRENGTHENING OXYGEN SYSTEMS IN ASIA AND THE PACIFIC

GUIDANCE NOTE

NOVEMBER 2022

ADB

ASIAN DEVELOPMENT BANK

© 2022 Asian Development Bank
6 ADB Avenue, Mandaluyong City, 1550 Metro Manila, Philippines
Tel +63 2 8632 4444; Fax +63 2 8636 2444
www.adb.org

Some rights reserved. Published in 2022.

ISBN 978-92-9269-792-1 (print); 978-92-9269-793-8 (electronic); 978-92-9269-794-5 (ebook)
Publication Stock No. TIM220490-2
DOI: http://dx.doi.org/10.22617/TIM220490-2

Note:
In this publication, "$" refers to United States dollars.

On the cover: The coronavirus disease (COVID-19) pandemic has underscored the importance of uninterrupted oxygen supply in medical facilities (photos by Jawad Jalali/ADB).

Cover design by Nonie Villanueva.

Contents

Tables, Figures, and Case Studies — v

Acknowledgments — vi

Abbreviations — vii

Executive Summary — viii

1 Introduction and Purpose — 1
Purpose of This Guidance Note — 1
Objectives — 1

2 Impact and Urgency of Improving Oxygen Systems — 2
The Life-Saving Impact of Oxygen — 3
Current Oxygen Gap — 5
COVID-19 Pandemic: Challenge and Opportunity — 5

3 Key Features of Oxygen Systems — 7
Systems Approach — 7

4 Clinical Use of Oxygen and Pulse Oximetry — 11
Oxygen and Hypoxemia — 12
Medical Oxygen Standards — 13
Delivery Devices — 14
Pulse Oximetry and the Health-Care Workforce — 16

5 Oxygen Production, Storage, and Distribution — 20
Summary of Oxygen Supply Options — 21
Oxygen Production — 24
Oxygen Storage and Distribution — 34

6 Measurement, Forecasting, and Planning   40
Measuring Oxygen Access   41
Forecasting Oxygen Need   44
Planning   46

7 Opportunities for Investment   50
Opportunities   50
Financing and Implementation Support   51
Leveraging COVID-19 Investments   52
Partnerships   53

8 Conclusions   55

9 Resources   57

Tables, Figures, and Case Studies

Tables

1	Pulse Oximeter Types and Use Cases	18
2	Summary of the Main Medical Oxygen Supply Options to Facilities and Patients	22
3	Summary of Most Useful Indicators of Oxygen Access	42
4	Opportunities for ADB Action to Support Country-Level Oxygen Systems Strengthening, Utilize Various Financing Mechanisms and Models, and Promote Knowledge Generation and Dissemination	51

Figures

1	Comparative Cost-Effectiveness of Child Pneumonia Interventions	4
2	Estimated Number of Patients with Hypoxemia Presenting to Facilities in Low- and Middle-Income Countries, 2021	6
3	Oxygen Systems at Different Levels of Health Service	8
4	Key Components of an Oxygen System	9
5	Oxygen Delivery Devices and Indicative Flow Rates and Inspired Oxygen Concentration	15
6	Pathways from Medical Oxygen Production to Distribution, Storage, and Clinical Use	21
7	Example Oxygen Cylinder Size and Capacity	37
8	Key Indicators for Measuring Oxygen Access	42
9	Oxygen Delivery Toolkit Resources Life Cycle	48
10	Percentage of Facilities in Indonesia by Province with Access to Oxygen, Heat Map	49
11	COVID-19 Access to COVID-19 Tools Accelerator	53

Case Studies

1	Uganda – Oxygen Systems Require Holistic Investment	9
2	Cambodia, Global – Oxygen and Pulse Oximetry Access to Health-Care Workers	19
3	Kenya – Hub-and-Spoke Model of Oxygen Supply	28
4	Malawi – Invest in Maintenance	30
5	Tonga – Oxygen for Remote Health Facilities	33
6	Global – Innovation in Piped Distribution Systems	39
7	Bangladesh – Integration of Oxygen Indicators in Health Information Systems	43
8	Global – Tools for Forecasting Needs and Planning	46
9	Global – Planning Steps and Tools, PATH Example	47
10	Indonesia – Procurement and Asset Management	49

Acknowledgments

Hamish R. Graham, consultant to the Asian Development Bank (ADB), prepared this guidance note. H. R. Graham is a senior research fellow at Murdoch Children's Research Institute (MCRI), University of Melbourne, Australia. The work was funded by the Sector and Thematic Training budget of the Sustainable Development and Climate Change Department (SDCC), coordinated by Health Sector Secretariat. The training materials, which included a staff seminar, were developed under the overall guidance of Arin Dutta, senior health specialist, SDCC.

The author is grateful for the feedback and perspectives provided by members of various United Nations agencies, governmental and nongovernment organizations, and private sector representatives, including Martha Gartley, Felix Lam, Damien Kirchhoffer, Jason Houdek, and Audrey Battu (Clinton Health Access Initiative); Lisa Smith and Elena Pantjushenko (PATH); Cindy McWhorter, Bev Bradley, Mansi Dalal, and Habtamu Tolla (United Nations Children's Fund [UNICEF] Supply Division); Alejandra Velez Ruiz Gaitan and Stefan Adriaenses (World Health Organization); Katerina Galluzzo and Robert Matiru (Unitaid); Adegoke Falade and Ayobami Bakare (University College Hospital Ibadan, Oxygen for Life Initiative); Shiellah Bagayana (FREO2 Foundation); Bernard Olayo (Center for Public Health and Development); Amy Gray, Trevor Duke, and Rami Subhi (MCRI, University of Melbourne); Eric McCollum (Johns Hopkins University); Steve Howie (University of Auckland); Carina King and Tim Baker (Karolinska Instituet); Sarah Sceery, Jim Ansara, Eric Buckley, and Steve Mtwea (Build Health International); Victoria Smith and Jim Stunkel (Assist International); Mireia Gil (Azimut 360 SCCL); and Leith Greenslade (Every Breath Counts coalition).

The authors also acknowledge the support of Michelle Apostol, associate health officer, and Benjamin Coghlan, senior health specialist, both of SDCC; as well as assistance from the publishing team in ADB's Department of Communications.

Abbreviations

ADB	Asian Development Bank
ASU	(cryogenic) air separation unit
BHI	Build Health International
BiPAP	bilevel positive airway pressure
CAPEX	capital expenditure
CHAI	Clinton Health Access Initiative
COVID-19	coronavirus disease
CPAP	continuous positive airway pressure
DHIS	district health information software
FiO$_2$	fraction of inspired oxygen
HFNC	high flow nasal cannula
ISO	International Organization for Standardization
LMIC	low- or middle-income country
LPM	liters per minute
Nm^3	normal cubic meter
OPEX	operational expenditure
PSA	pressure swing adsorption
SpO$_2$	peripheral capillary oxygen saturation
UNICEF	United Nations Children's Fund
VIE	vacuum-insulated evaporator
VSA	vacuum swing adsorption
WHO	World Health Organization

Executive Summary

This guidance note provides a **comprehensive look at medical oxygen ecosystems** with a focus on strategies to strengthen systems for the benefit of patients beyond the novel coronavirus disease (COVID-19) pandemic. It describes the key components of oxygen systems and highlights challenges and needs from medical oxygen supply to patient use, and discusses the role of the Asian Development Bank (ADB) in supporting countries to strengthen oxygen systems for the medium and long term.

Medical oxygen is an essential medicine required for a broad range of clinical needs including pneumonia, COVID-19 and other respiratory illnesses; stabilization and care for patients with trauma, sepsis, or other severe illnesses; care for small and sick newborns; and obstetrics, surgical, and anesthetic procedures.

Oxygen services are essential at every level of the health system, but their scope will vary. At smaller facilities, the priority is pulse oximetry and simple oxygen supplies to identify, stabilize, and transport severely ill patients. At larger facilities, the needs include continuous oxygen administration for a variety of patients using simple and more advanced respiratory care devices.

Oxygen systems strengthening at the district hospital level has been shown to be a cost-effective child health strategy, reducing hospital deaths from pneumonia by 50% and all-cause mortality by 25%. Cost-effectiveness of oxygen systems strengthening has not been measured for other populations, but clearly the benefits reach a broad population of patients.

Effective oxygen systems strengthening requires a systems approach, addressing challenges to oxygen supply and distribution, and how it is used for patients. The COVID-19 pandemic has highlighted, and exacerbated, current deficiencies including poor coordination of oxygen supply and distribution; lack of data to inform decision-making; inadequate financing; weak repair and maintenance systems; and lack of pulse oximetry and guidelines to guide oxygen use.

There is currently unprecedented opportunity for collaboration between governments, funders, and implementing partners to
   (i)   Coordinate oxygen systems planning, procurement, distribution, and maintenance at a larger scale and use data better for planning, monitoring, and improving systems.
   (ii) Increase supply of bulk oxygen in areas that struggle from limited supply options or competition and improve the distribution of oxygen to populations that have been historically neglected.
   (iii) Strengthen maintenance, repair, and biomedical capacity for oxygen and imagine better systems to keep equipment functioning longer.
   (iv) Support health-care workers with the tools and skills to use pulse oximetry and oxygen better.
   (v)   Use financial tools to de-risk and enable innovative oxygen supply, distribution and use models, and leverage off other investments (e.g., COVID-19).

The COVID-19 pandemic has shone a spotlight on the human cost of weak oxygen systems and destroyed any remaining excuses for inaction. The tasks involved in strengthening oxygen systems are not complex and will have broad benefits to health systems, health services, and end users. However, they require cooperation between governments, funders, implementers, and those providing technical support.

This guidance note provides some ideas and resources to progress work in the Asia and Pacific region, including specific opportunities for ADB support. And it contains hope that the grim lessons from the current crisis will catalyze the collective political will and ambition needed to achieve oxygen access to the very last mile.

1 Introduction and Purpose

Purpose of This Guidance Note

This guidance note has been prepared to guide Asian Development Bank (ADB) staff, health managers, and policy makers in the Asia and Pacific region to understand key aspects of a medical oxygen ecosystem, recognize common deficiencies and weaknesses, and identify opportunities to build more effective and sustainable systems. This will also be useful to funders or financiers, policy makers, and health managers in other regions, particularly the African region.

Objectives

To understand the **key components of the medical oxygen ecosystem**, including infrastructure for production, mechanisms for supply and delivery, components and systems for appropriate use, health-care worker and technician capacity, and coordination and leadership.

To understand the **key weaknesses in existing oxygen systems**, and the consequences of oxygen inaccessibility at different levels of the health system and in different need situations (e.g., acute need such as coronavirus disease (COVID-2019) peaks, and as routine yet critical needs at other times).

To understand in general **what is needed to plan for a sustainable medical oxygen ecosystem** in the medium to long term, with an emphasis on a health systems-strengthening approach to oxygen production, distribution, and use.

To explore the role for **ADB in collaboration with governments and other partners** in supporting oxygen systems improvements in the Asia and Pacific region, and globally.

2 Impact and Urgency of Improving Oxygen Systems

Key Messages

✅ **Oxygen services are essential** for the care of newborns, children, adolescents, and adults and have been an integral component of clinical guidelines for over a century.

✅ **Oxygen systems strengthening is life-saving and cost-effective,** reducing the risk of death among hospitalized children by one-quarter, and comparing favorably with the most cost-effective child pneumonia interventions—and benefiting many other children and adults.

✅ **Oxygen systems have been a neglected priority** in global health strategies, financing, and advocacy. The COVID-19 pandemic has exposed deficiencies in existing oxygen systems and offered an opportunity to build back better for the long term.

✅ **Existing oxygen systems challenges** include poor coordination of oxygen supply and distribution; lack of data to inform decision-making; inadequate financing (particularly for ongoing operational needs); weak repair and maintenance systems; and lack of pulse oximeters and protocols to guide oxygen use. These weaknesses result in failure to identify patients who need oxygen, lack of adequate oxygen supplies to meet need, excessive cost to patients (and health facilities), and excess mortality.

The Life-Saving Impact of Oxygen

Oxygen has been a standard of care for over a century with effectiveness in treating respiratory conditions established well before the randomized controlled trial era.[1] As such, the clinical use of oxygen (including the use of pulse oximetry to measure blood oxygen levels) is an integral part of clinical care and guidelines for **newborns, children, adolescents, and adults**.[2]

In the past 2 decades, many small- and medium-scale programs have sought to improve oxygen systems.[3] The most effective approaches have taken a systems approach—involving oxygen equipment; education for technicians and health-care workers; and broader improvements of infrastructure (e.g., power), management, and care processes (e.g., quality improvement teams).[4]

Impact on Child Pneumonia Mortality

A meta-analysis of recent oxygen improvement programs found that improving hospital oxygen systems was associated with a 48% reduction in hospital pneumonia mortality among children under 5 years of age, and a 26% reduction in all-cause under-5 mortality.[5] The cost-effectiveness of these programs on child pneumonia ranged from $1,465 to $7,410 per life saved, or $44 to $225 per disability-adjusted life year saved—comparing very favorably with the most cost-effective pneumonia interventions (Figure 1).[6]

These cost-effectiveness estimates concur with previous modeling estimates that suggested increased availability and use of pulse oximetry, when oxygen supplies are available, could save 148,000 child pneumonia deaths annually in 15 high-mortality countries,[7] and could benefit thousands more severely ill patients through better recognition, referral, and management.[8] Based on these data, oxygen systems improvements will be integrated into the Lives Saved Tool,[9] a mathematical model that estimates the impact of changing coverage of key interventions on mortality in low- and middle-income countries (LMICs).

1   J. E. Heffner. 2013. The Story of Oxygen. *Respiratory Care*. 58(1). pp. 18–31. doi: 10.4187/respcare.01831.
2   World Health Organization (WHO). 2011. *IMAI District Clinican Manual: Hospital Care for Adolescents and Adults*. Geneva; WHO. 2013. *Pocket Book of Hospital Care for Children: Guidelines for the Management of Common Childhood Illnesses*. 2nd ed. Geneva: WHO. 2014. *Integrated Management of Childhood Illness - Chart Booklet*. Geneva.
3   H. R. Graham et al. 2017. Providing Oxygen to Children in Hospitals: A Realist Review. *Bulletin of the World Health Organization*. 95(4). pp. 288–302. doi: 10.2471/blt.16.186676.
4   F. Lam et al. 2021. Oxygen Systems Strengthening as an Intervention to Prevent Childhood Deaths Due to Pneumonia in Low-Resource Settings: Systematic Review, Meta-Analysis, and Cost-Effectiveness. *BMJ Global Health*.
5   L. Niessen et al. 2009. Comparative Impact Assessment of Child Pneumonia Interventions. *Bulletin of the World Health Organization*. 87(6). pp. 472–480.
6   A. J. Enoch, M. English, and S. Shepperd. 2016. Does Pulse Oximeter Use Impact Health Outcomes? A Systematic Review. *Archives of Disease in Childhood*. 101(8). pp. 694–00. doi: 10.1136/archdischild-2015-309638.
7   15 countries: Afghanistan, Bangladesh, Burkina Faso, Democratic Republic of the Congo (DRC), Ethiopia, India, Indonesia, Kenya, Mali, Niger, Nigeria, Pakistan, Sudan, Somalia, and Uganda.
8   H. R. Graham et al. 2021. Oxygen Systems and Quality of Care for Children with Pneumonia, Malaria and Diarrhoea: Analysis of a Stepped-Wedge Trial in Nigeria. *PLoS ONE*. 16(7):e0254229. doi: 10.1371/journal.pone.0254229 [published online first: 9 July 2021].
9   The Lives Saved Tool. https://www.livessavedtool.org/.

Figure 1: Comparative Cost-Effectiveness of Child Pneumonia Interventions

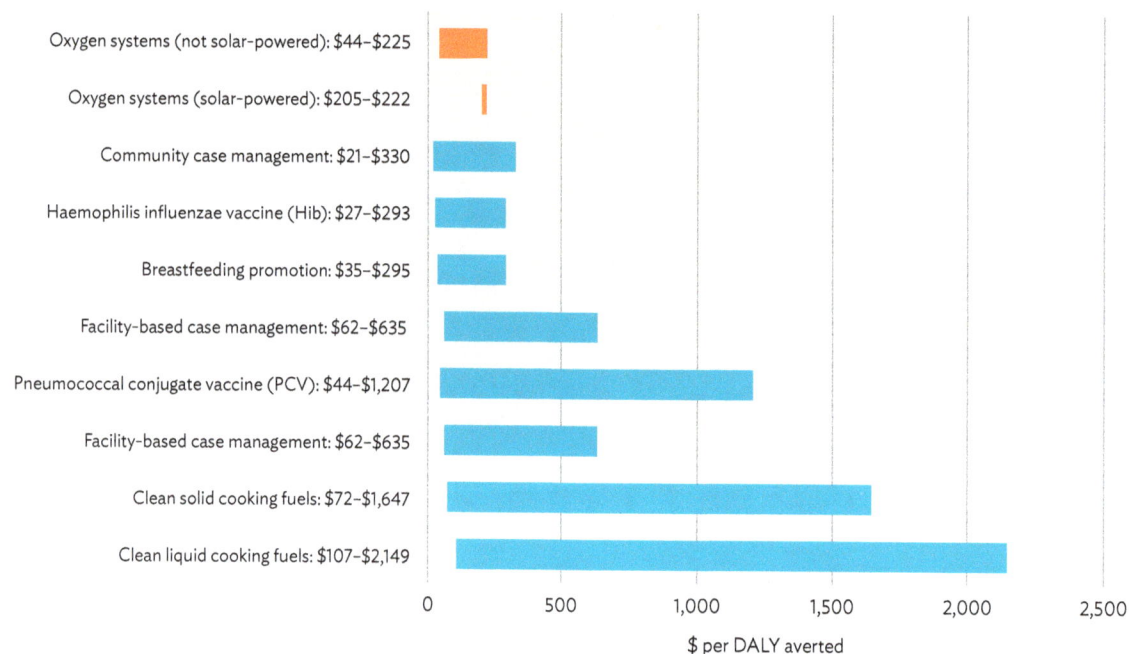

Intervention	$ per DALY averted
Oxygen systems (not solar-powered): $44–$225	
Oxygen systems (solar-powered): $205–$222	
Community case management: $21–$330	
Haemophilis influenzae vaccine (Hib): $27–$293	
Breastfeeding promotion: $35–$295	
Facility-based case management: $62–$635	
Pneumococcal conjugate vaccine (PCV): $44–$1,207	
Facility-based case management: $62–$635	
Clean solid cooking fuels: $72–$1,647	
Clean liquid cooking fuels: $107–$2,149	

DALY = disability-adjusted life year.
Sources: Adapted from F. Lam et al. 2021. Oxygen Systems Strengthening as an Intervention to Prevent Childhood Deaths Due to Pneumonia in Low-Resource Settings: Systematic Review, Meta-Analysis, and Cost-Effectiveness. *BMJ Global Health*; with comparisons to L. Niessen et al. 2009. Comparative Impact Assessment of Child Pneumonia Interventions. *Bulletin of the World Health Organization.* 87(6). pp. 472–480.

Impact on Other Populations and Conditions

However, while these data are impressive, they underestimate overall cost-effectiveness as they focused on the impact on children under-5 with pneumonia—not the broader population of newborns, children, and adults, who also benefited from the improved systems. These data also only included hospital-level oxygen improvement interventions using oxygen concentrator-based solutions, with no data available on the cost-effectiveness of broader health systems-level approaches or the use of larger-scale oxygen supply technologies (i.e., liquid oxygen or oxygen plants).

Other evidence shows that the introduction of pulse oximetry and oxygen supplies improves quality of care, including assessment of severity, decisions about referral and management, and may influence resource allocation (e.g., time spent in triage) (footnotes 6 and 8). The clinical and economic implications of these aspects of oxygen systems remain to be evaluated.

Current Oxygen Gap

Effective **oxygen systems strengthening requires a systems approach**, addressing challenges in oxygen supply and distribution and how it is used for patients. Unfortunately, oxygen systems have been poorly financed and managed, with weaknesses that were hidden to most of the global community until the COVID-19 pandemic—but painfully evident to patients and health-care workers in LMICs.

Health-care workers, technicians, and hospital administrators in many countries have encountered oxygen systems weaknesses as a daily headache for decades. These endemic challenges include (i) poor coordination of oxygen supply and distribution; (ii) lack of data to inform decision-making; (iii) inadequate financing (particularly for ongoing operational needs); (iv) weak repair and maintenance systems; and (v) lack of pulse oximeters and protocols to guide oxygen use.

These weaknesses result in failure to identify patients who need oxygen, lack of adequate oxygen supplies to meet need, excessive cost to patients (and health facilities), and excess mortality. The oxygen gap is typically worse in smaller facilities and more remote areas, and in poorer regions with weaker health systems. The underlying oxygen systems deficiencies are often missed in routine facility readiness assessments which typically only ask about the presence of oxygen supply equipment and do not evaluate function, adequacy to meet patient need, or how pulse oximeters or oxygen are used clinically (see Measuring Oxygen Access).

Coordinated, long-term strengthening of oxygen systems is essential to improving clinical care, outcomes, and human development in many LMICs.

COVID-19 Pandemic: Challenge and Opportunity

The COVID-19 pandemic has highlighted and exacerbated existing weaknesses in oxygen systems. The hallmark features of COVID-19 are acute respiratory failure resulting in low blood oxygen (hypoxemia) and requiring oxygen administration with or without higher level respiratory support. These features are like other causes of pneumonia, but there are three factors that have made the impact on oxygen systems more marked. First, COVID-19 has disproportionately affected adults (rather than children) who require far greater volumes of oxygen than similarly unwell children. Second, COVID-19 respiratory failure often requires long periods of respiratory support (weeks rather than days). Third, COVID-19 has affected communities in waves, in some cases, overwhelming hospitals with greater need for oxygen in a single month than they usually require in a year.

The impact of COVID-19 on oxygen need has been visualized in the COVID-19 Oxygen Needs Tracker,[10] updated daily with data extrapolated from COVID-19 case numbers reported to the World Health Organization (WHO). However, while COVID-19 waves have been responsible for tragic and highly visible failures of oxygen systems in many countries, it accounts for a minority of global oxygen need. Indeed, the sharp rises in oxygen need for COVID-19 have come on top of a greater baseline oxygen need for newborns, children, and adults who need oxygen for a variety of reasons: acute respiratory illness, sepsis, other critical care needs, newborn care, resuscitation, childbirth, surgery, anesthesia, and more.

---

10   COVID-19 Oxygen Needs Tracker.

Unpublished estimates from the Clinton Health Access Initiative (CHAI) and the Murdoch Children's Research Institute suggest that there were 73 million people with hypoxemia attending health facilities in LMIC in 2021 (Figure 2). This included adults and children with pneumonia, sepsis, trauma, and other severe illnesses; and newborns with infection or born prematurely. It did not include all those who need oxygen for other reasons, such as resuscitation, or during anesthesia for surgery or childbirth.

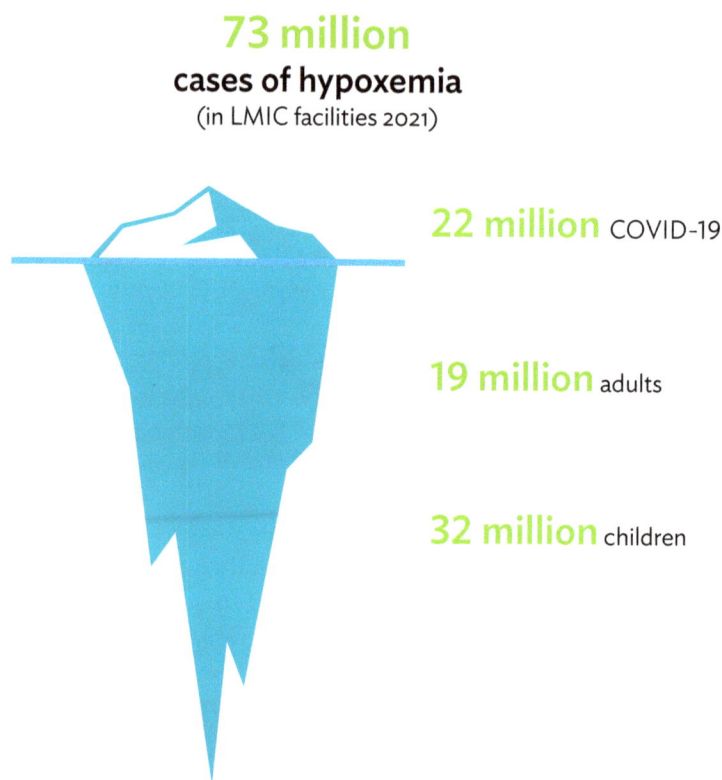

Figure 2: Estimated Number of Patients with Hypoxemia Presenting to Facilities in Low- and Middle-Income Countries, 2021

73 million
cases of hypoxemia
(in LMIC facilities 2021)

22 million COVID-19

19 million adults

32 million children

COVID-19 = coronavirus disease, LMIC = low- and middle-income country.
Source: Image provided by author from unpublished estimates by H. Graham and F. Lam in 2022.

3 Key Features of Oxygen Systems

Key Messages

✅ **Oxygen systems** include the equipment, people, and processes to produce oxygen, store and distribute oxygen to facilities (and to the points of care within facilities), maintain and repair equipment, deliver oxygen safely and effectively to patients (including monitoring), and provide coordinated oversight.

✅ **Oxygen services** are relevant to all levels of the health system, but what they look like will vary. The appropriate design and structure of an oxygen system depends on the facilities served, existing oxygen infrastructure, accessibility of particular equipment and technical support, and geographic and contextual factors.

✅ **Oxygen systems strengthening must take a systems approach,** considering the appropriate technology mix, service delivery systems, workforce support, and financing mechanisms to fit the particular context.

Systems Approach

Oxygen systems include the *equipment*, *people*, and *processes* to *produce* oxygen, *store* and *distribute* oxygen to facilities (and to the points of care within facilities), *maintain* and *repair* equipment, *deliver* oxygen safely and effectively to patients (including monitoring), and provide *coordinated oversight*.[11]

---

11   WHO and United Nations Children's Fund (UNICEF). 2019. *WHO-UNICEF Technical Specifications and Guidance for Oxygen Therapy Devices*. Geneva: WHO.

There is not a single "best" design of an oxygen system and the most appropriate technology mix and system design will depend on local factors such as (i) the number and size of facilities being serviced; (ii) the populations served (e.g., geography, epidemiology); (iii) access to technology and technical expertise; (iv) the state of existing infrastructure and systems; and (v) financing mechanisms.

Oxygen systems are relevant to all levels of the health system, but their applications will vary (Figure 3). For example, at primary care level, facilities may primarily require pulse oximetry and emergency oxygen services to identify and stabilize severely unwell patients prior to transporting them to a higher-level health facility. In contrast, hospitals typically require comprehensive oxygen services for multiple service areas, including for emergency care, inpatient management of severely ill patients, and surgical care. Facilities with intensive care service capacity and high surgical demand will have specialized requirements for oxygen supply, distribution, and use.

Careful consideration of all the critical elements of an oxygen system is essential to achieving effective outcomes and optimizing efficiency (Figure 4). Too often, investments are made in one aspect of oxygen systems (e.g., increasing oxygen supply by construction of new oxygen plants) without adequately addressing other limitations in oxygen supply, distribution, and use. This will not only fail to deliver intended outcomes, but may rapidly erode the investments made (Case Study 1).

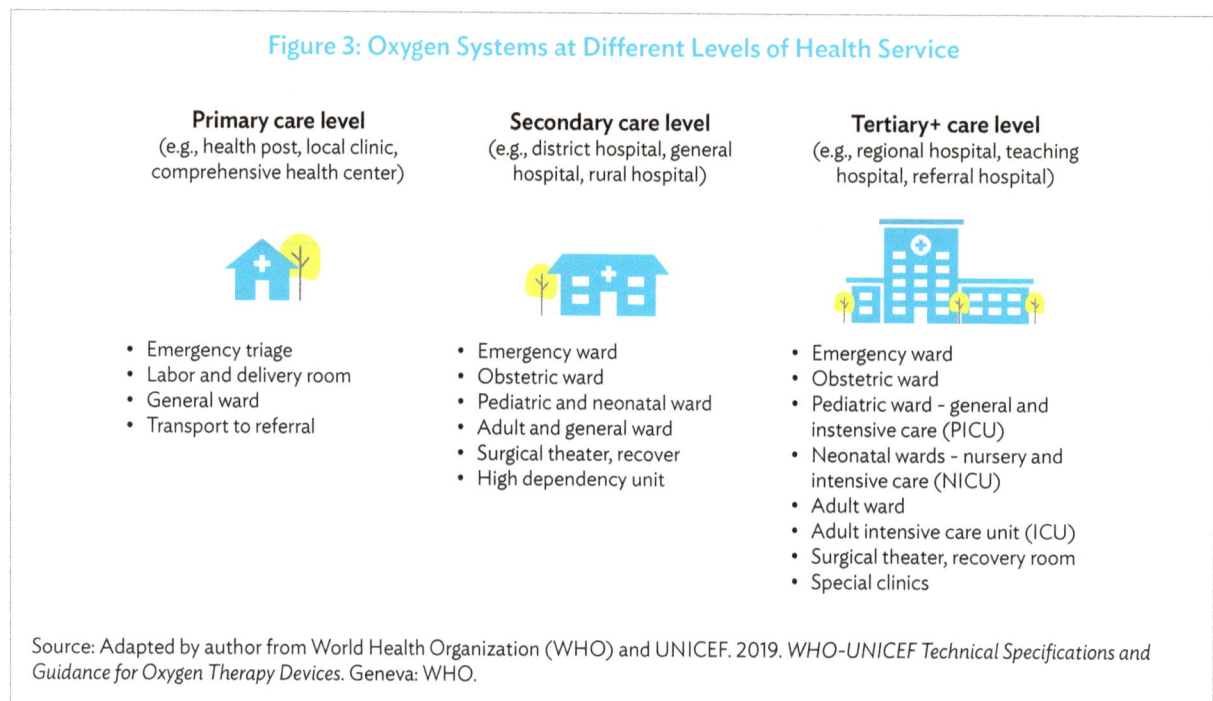

Figure 3: Oxygen Systems at Different Levels of Health Service

Primary care level
(e.g., health post, local clinic, comprehensive health center)

- Emergency triage
- Labor and delivery room
- General ward
- Transport to referral

Secondary care level
(e.g., district hospital, general hospital, rural hospital)

- Emergency ward
- Obstetric ward
- Pediatric and neonatal ward
- Adult and general ward
- Surgical theater, recover
- High dependency unit

Tertiary+ care level
(e.g., regional hospital, teaching hospital, referral hospital)

- Emergency ward
- Obstetric ward
- Pediatric ward - general and instensive care (PICU)
- Neonatal wards - nursery and intensive care (NICU)
- Adult ward
- Adult intensive care unit (ICU)
- Surgical theater, recovery room
- Special clinics

Source: Adapted by author from World Health Organization (WHO) and UNICEF. 2019. *WHO-UNICEF Technical Specifications and Guidance for Oxygen Therapy Devices*. Geneva: WHO.

Figure 4: Key Components of an Oxygen System

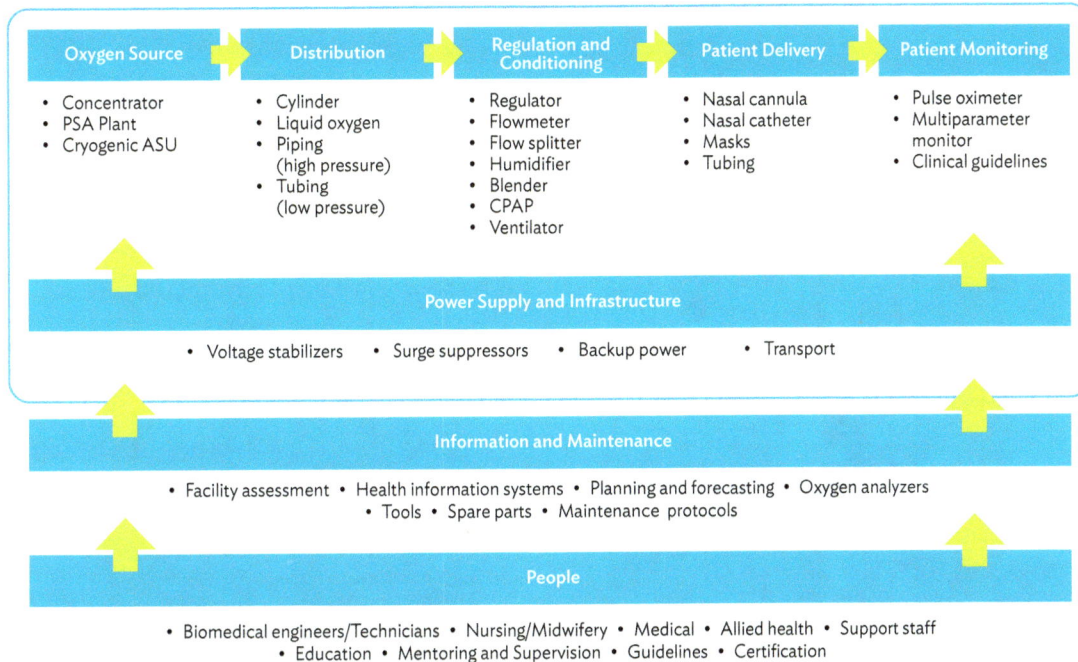

Oxygen Source	Distribution	Regulation and Conditioning	Patient Delivery	Patient Monitoring
• Concentrator • PSA Plant • Cryogenic ASU	• Cylinder • Liquid oxygen • Piping (high pressure) • Tubing (low pressure)	• Regulator • Flowmeter • Flow splitter • Humidifier • Blender • CPAP • Ventilator	• Nasal cannula • Nasal catheter • Masks • Tubing	• Pulse oximeter • Multiparameter monitor • Clinical guidelines

Power Supply and Infrastructure

• Voltage stabilizers   • Surge suppressors   • Backup power   • Transport

Information and Maintenance

• Facility assessment • Health information systems • Planning and forecasting • Oxygen analyzers
• Tools • Spare parts • Maintenance protocols

People

• Biomedical engineers/Technicians • Nursing/Midwifery • Medical • Allied health • Support staff
• Education • Mentoring and Supervision • Guidelines • Certification

ASU = air separation unit, CPAP = continuous positive airway pressure, PSA = pressure swing adsorption.
Source: Adapted by author from World Health Organization (WHO) and UNICEF. 2019. *WHO-UNICEF Technical Specifications and Guidance for Oxygen Therapy Devices*. Geneva: WHO.

CASE STUDY 1

Uganda – Oxygen Systems Require Holistic Investment

The Government of Uganda was among the first countries to develop a national oxygen scale-up plan, providing a holistic approach to improving oxygen access that address supply, distribution, and use issues.[12] In developing the plan, the government identified that recent major capital investments in oxygen were being undermined by other systemic limitations and not delivering the anticipated return on investment.

For example, Uganda had invested substantially in building oxygen plants at all regional referral hospitals with the intention that these would produce oxygen to be distributed to the hospitals and all other hospitals and major health centers in their catchment areas. However, oxygen plants were unable to produce to capacity due to irregular power supply and lack of staffing outside daylight hours; no means to distribute cylinders to smaller facilities; and health-care workers continued to use oxygen without pulse oximetry or guidance. Recognizing these challenges, the government is working on implementing its oxygen scale-up plan holistically, investing in optimization of oxygen plant function, improving information and distribution systems, and building technical and health-care worker capacity (footnote 12).

Continued on next page

---

12   Ministry of Health-Uganda. 2018. *National Scale Up of Medical Oxygen Implementation Plan*. Kampala, Uganda: Ministry of Health.

Case Study 1 continued

Uganda Ministry of Health Oxygen Scale-Up Plan. Pressure swing adsorption plant installed in the Regional Referral Hospital in Uganda (photo by Hamish Graham).

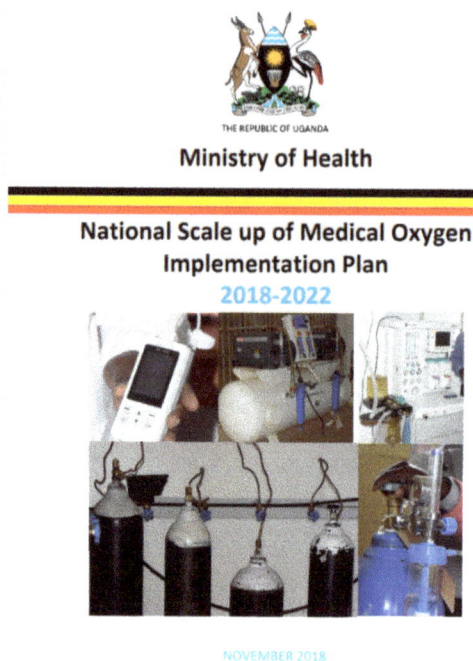

The following sections describe some of the technology, personnel, information, and practical considerations for oxygen systems. For consistency, the information is divided into information (i) **clinical use of oxygen and pulse oximetry,** (ii) **oxygen production,** and (iii) **oxygen storage and distribution.** Comments on power supply and infrastructure, maintenance, and people (health care and technical workforce) are integrated within these areas and there is a dedicated section on **measurement, forecasting, and planning**.

Please refer to Resources for additional information, including the PATH/CHAI *Oxygen Generation and Storage series*[13] for a more complete summary of oxygen-related equipment and WHO technical specifications[14] for technical details.

---

[13]   PATH and Clinton Health Access Initiative (CHAI). 2021. *Oxygen Generation and Storage*. Seattle: PATH, CHAI.

[14]   WHO and UNICEF. 2019. *WHO-UNICEF Technical Specifications and Guidance for Oxygen Therapy Devices*. Geneva: WHO; WHO. 2015. Technical Specifications for Oxygen Concentrators. In WHO, ed. *WHO Medical Device Technical Series*. Geneva; WHO. 2020. *Priority Medical Devices List for the COVID-19 Response and Associated Technical Specifications: Interim Guidance*. 19 November. Geneva.

4 Clinical Use of Oxygen and Pulse Oximetry

Key Messages

✅ **Oxygen is an essential medicine** for severely unwell patients, safe surgery, and anesthesia; and an essential service required in any health facility providing this care. Pulse oximetry is an essential tool to detect hypoxemia and assess and monitor severely unwell patients.

✅ **Medical oxygen** must contain at least 82% oxygen (compared with 21% oxygen in air) and global standards distinguish between oxygen produced cryogenically versus pressure or vacuum swing adsorption by defining Oxygen 99% and Oxygen 93% standards. There is negligible clinical difference between 85%, 90%, 95%, or 99% oxygen, as oxygen is almost always mixed with air to achieve a lower inspired oxygen concentration before reaching the patient's lungs. However, the choice of oxygen supply may have practical and regulatory implications for health service systems.

✅ **Oxygen delivery devices** are selected by health-care workers following guidelines based on the patient's illness severity, age, and size—with most patients requiring simple low-flow oxygen. Oxygen delivery devices may range from simple (e.g., nasal cannulae or masks) to complex (e.g., ventilator circuit), and most can run from any oxygen source.

✅ **Pulse oximetry** is the key to identifying hypoxemia, guiding oxygen therapy, and achieving effective oxygen systems. Using pulse oximetry and oxygen properly requires skilled and motivated health-care workers. Pulse oximeters range in cost and quality, with handheld devices offering the best value for money for most use cases.

Oxygen and Hypoxemia

Oxygen is a natural gas that is essential for human life. Deprivation of oxygen to our body's cells quickly causes cell damage, proceeding to irreversible organ damage and death. Humans extract oxygen from ambient air through breathing (respiration), through which red blood cells in our lungs exchange oxygen for carbon dioxide (gas exchange). Red blood cells then carry oxygen molecules throughout our body (circulation) where they are used by cells to release energy (metabolism) to function.

Blood oxygen level can be measured from gas analysis on a blood sample (partial pressure of oxygen in blood [PaO_2]) or noninvasively using a **pulse oximeter** (peripheral capillary oxygen saturation [SpO_2]). In healthy individuals, SpO_2 is typically >97% (although it can be lower in people living at high altitude who physiologically adapt to the low oxygen environment). **Hypoxemia** is conventionally defined as SpO_2 <90% (or PaO_2 <60 mmHg) and requires prompt identification and treatment with oxygen therapy.[15]

Hypoxemia is deadly, increasing the risk of death four to seven times in acutely unwell patients. Even moderate hypoxemia (SpO_2 <94%) is associated with increased risk of death[16] and is an indication for oxygen therapy in particular risk groups (e.g., severe anemia, brain injury).[17]

Hypoxemia is common among acutely unwell newborns, children, and adults. While hypoxemia is particularly common among those with respiratory conditions such as pneumonia, it can also be associated with many other illnesses that do not primarily affect the lungs, including severe malaria, sepsis, meningitis, and cardiac abnormalities.[18] Global estimates suggest that 46 million unwell patients present to health facilities in LMICs with hypoxemia annually, approximately half of whom are newborns and children. The COVID-19 pandemic accounted for a substantial proportion of this demand, with around 8 million with hypoxemia in 2020.

Hypoxemia is also a deadly risk of surgery, including for obstetric complications, trauma, and during anesthesia for nonurgent procedures. Pulse oximetry and oxygen are, therefore, core components of safe surgery and anesthesia,[19] used for a substantial proportion of the 300 million surgical procedures required worldwide annually.[20]

---

15 WHO. 2016. *Oxygen Therapy for Children*. Geneva; S. Namasopo et al. 2014. Solar-Powered Oxygen Delivery. *American Journal of Tropical Medicine and Hygiene*. 2 (1). p. 15.

16 H. R. Graham et al. 2019. Hypoxaemia in Hospitalised Children and Neonates: A Prospective Cohort Study in Nigerian Secondary-Level Hospitals. *eClinicalMedicine*. doi: https://doi.org/10.1016/j.eclinm.2019.10.009.

17 WHO. 2016. *Oxygen Therapy for Children*. Geneva.

18 H. R. Graham et al. 2019. Hypoxaemia in Hospitalised Children and Neonates: A Prospective Cohort Study in Nigerian Secondary-Level Hospitals. *eClinicalMedicine*. doi: https://doi.org/10.1016/j.eclinm.2019.10.009; R. Subhi et al. 2009. The Prevalence of Hypoxaemia among Ill Children in Developing Countries: A Systematic Review. *The Lancet Infectious Diseases*. 9(4). pp. 219–227. doi: http://dx.doi.org/10.1016/S1473-3099%2809%2970071-4.

19 A. Enright et al. 2016. Lifebox: A Global Patient Safety Initiative. *A&A Case Reports*. 6(12). pp. 366–369. doi: 10.1213/XAA.0000000000000335; A. C. Kwok et al. 2013. Implementation of the World Health Organization Surgical Safety Checklist, Including Introduction of Pulse Oximetry, in a Resource-Limited Setting. *Annals of Surgery*. 257(4). pp. 633–639. doi: 10.1097/SLA.0b013e3182777fa4.

20 J. G. Meara et al. 2015. Global Surgery 2030: Evidence and Solutions for Achieving Health, Welfare, and Economic Development. *The Lancet*. 386(9993). pp. 569–624. doi: 10.1016/s0140-6736(15)60160-x.

Medical Oxygen Standards

WHO lists medical oxygen as an essential medicine[21] and pulse oximeters as a priority medical device.[22] Prior to 2017, the WHO list only included oxygen as an inhalational medicine in general anesthesia, and many country essential medicines' lists reflected this narrow indication. After a concerted effort by members of the medical and global health community, WHO updated the list to include oxygen as an essential medicine for the management of hypoxemia.[23]

WHO guidelines define medical oxygen as containing a minimum 82% oxygen and free from any contamination, generated by an oil-free compressor. In comparison, ambient air contains approximately 21% oxygen, 78% nitrogen, 1% argon, and a small fraction of carbon dioxide and other gases.

In clinical use, medical oxygen is mixed with air before reaching the lungs because high concentrations of oxygen are potentially toxic.[24] The concentration of oxygen reaching the lungs is called the fraction of inspired oxygen (FiO_2). When oxygen is provided using simple noninvasive respiratory support (e.g., nasal prongs, face masks, nasal catheters), patients breathe in both oxygen and air resulting in an FiO_2 ~25%–50% depending on the oxygen flow rate and the volume of the patient's respiration. When oxygen is provided in more advanced respiratory support (e.g., continuous positive airway pressure (CPAP), mechanical ventilation), clinicians set the air–oxygen mix to provide a certain FiO_2 (typically not greater than 50, but can be higher if needed).

Standards for medical oxygen largely focus on oxygen purity. The earliest standards were drafted over 50 years ago and covered oxygen produced by cryogenic distillation, specifying a minimum oxygen content of 99%. More recent updates to standards have included oxygen produced pressure swing adsorption (PSA) or vacuum swing adsorption (VSA) specifying an oxygen content of 90%–96%.

For example, the European Pharmacopoeia (Ph. Eur.) currently includes two monographs on oxygen: *Oxygen (0417)* and *Oxygen (93%) (2455)*,[25] and considered adding a third *Oxygen (98%) (3098)* to cover oxygen made by more advanced PSA methods capable of producing oxygen with a nominal oxygen content of 98%.[26]

In 2021, WHO followed the European Pharmacopoeia in adding Oxygen 93% to its current listing in the *International Pharmacopoeia*.[27] This update will be consistent with the European Pharmacopoeia (footnote 25), United States Pharmacopeia,[28] International Organization for Standardization (ISO) Standards,[29] and the WHO technical specifications for oxygen devices (footnote 11), oxygen concentrators,[30] and PSA oxygen plants.[31]

21   A. Enright et al. 2016. Lifebox: A Global Patient Safety Initiative. *A&A Case Reports*. 6(12). pp. 366–369. doi: 10.1213/XAA.0000000000000335.

22   A. C. Kwok et al. 2013. Implementation of the World Health Organization Surgical Safety Checklist, Including Introduction of Pulse Oximetry, in a Resource-Limited Setting. *Annals of Surgery*. 257(4). pp. 633–639. doi: 10.1097/SLA.0b013e3182777fa4.

23   Path. 2017. *New WHO Designation for Oxygen Could Save Thousands of Lives Globally*. 17 June 2017. https://www.path.org/media-center/new-who-designation-for-oxygen-could-save-thousands-of-lives-globally/.

24   In at-risk populations (e.g., preterm newborns) health-care workers set a target saturation range to prevent both hypoxemia and hyperoxemia.

25   Council of Europe, European Pharmacopoeia Commission, and European Directorate for the Quality of Medicines & Healthcare. 2019. *European Pharmacopoeia*. 10th ed. Council of Europe.

26   Council of Europe Newsroom. 2020. *Oxygen 98%: Ph. Eur. Receives Valuable Feedback on New Oxygen Quality*. Strasbourg, France: Council of Europe.

27   WHO. 2021. Medicinal Oxygen (Oxygenium Medicinalis): Draft proposal for revision in The International Pharmacopoeia (July 2021). Working document QAS/20867/Rev2. Geneva.

28   Convention USP. 2020. *The United States Pharmacopeia*. The National Formulary. Rockville (MD), US: United States Pharmacopeial Convention.

29   International Organization for Standardization (ISO). 2016. ISO 7396-1:2016. *Medical Gas Pipeline Systems — Part 1: Pipeline Systems for Compressed Medical Gases and Vacuum*. Geneva.

30   WHO. 2015. Technical Specifications for Oxygen Concentrators. In WHO, ed. *WHO Medical Device Technical Series*. Geneva.

31   WHO. 2020. *Technical Specifications for Pressure Swing Adsorption (PSA) Oxygen Plants: Interim Guidance*. Geneva.

Importantly, the clinical application of oxygen is no different whether it is of 85%, 90%, 95%, or 99% oxygen purity.[27] It makes no difference to the ability of hemoglobin to bind oxygen, and the additional amount of oxygen is practically irrelevant as it is mixed with air before reaching the lungs. Standard respiratory care devices need minimal to no modification if using oxygen <99% and the very few devices that would be compromised are typically only available in high-resourced intensive care settings (e.g., ventilators using oxygen analyzers with internal automatic oxygen calibration).[32]

When the European Standards were updated in 2010, health-care providers and managers welcomed the opportunity to diversify oxygen supplies—particularly in more rural geographies and for military or mobile application (footnote 32). However, there may be practical and regulatory challenges to overcome relating to legal liability, integrity of piped systems, and optimized function of respiratory care devices (footnote 32).

Anecdotal information suggests that there is substantial misinformation about the implications of medical oxygen of different purity, and a recent investigation by the Bureau of Investigative Journalism revealed evidence that some liquid oxygen companies have pressured hospitals against installation of PSA plants with false claims that oxygen produced by this method is dangerous to patient health.[33]

Delivery Devices

Oxygen is delivered to patients using a variety of delivery devices ranging from low-flow delivery via nasal prongs or face masks to higher-flow delivery through tight-fitting masks and endotracheal tubes (Figure 5).

Most patients will require low-flow oxygen through nasal cannulae (prongs), nasal catheters, or face masks. These devices allow patients to breath in air (21% oxygen) alongside supplemental oxygen, increasing the concentration of oxygen delivered to their lungs to around 25% to 60% (though this can be increased further by adding a reservoir bag). Health-care workers can adjust the flow rates based on the clinical situation. These low-flow oxygen delivery devices can be used by low-level health-care workers with appropriate clinical guidelines and require minimal care or maintenance.

Higher levels of respiratory support typically combine supplemental oxygen with higher gas flow or pressure. These include high-flow (HFNC) and continuous or bilevel positive airway pressure (CPAP or BiPAP), as well as invasive ventilation. These require specialized machines and patient interfaces to deliver air or oxygen mix through the nose, mouth, or directly to the trachea. These devices typically require health-care workers to set the desired concentration of oxygen intended to reach the lungs (FiO_2) and adjust it based on the clinical situation.

HFNC, BiPAP, CPAP, and ventilators must be operated by highly skilled health-care workers and require regular care and maintenance (specific needs will depend on their complexity). Some devices will have components, such as humidifiers that need to be cleaned and disinfected between patients.

Oxygen delivery interfaces must be sized appropriately to the patient—typically differing markedly between newborns, children, and adults. Most oxygen delivery interfaces are single use, disposable, and low cost (e.g., nasal cannulae and simple masks <1 each). However, many can be cleaned, disinfected, and reused safely—and this is particularly relevant where there are limited supplies or low capacity to pay.

---

32   T. Prien et al. 2014. Oxygen 93: A New Option for European Hospitals. *British Journal of Anaesthesia*. 113(5). pp. 886–867. doi: 10.1093/bja/aeu358 [published online first: 19 October 2014].

33   M. Davies, L. Rios, and C. Giles. 2021. Oxygen Firms Accused of Intimidating Mexican Hospitals during Pandemic. *The Guardian*.

Most oxygen delivery devices will work perfectly well from any oxygen source (piped, cylinder, concentrator), at any pressure, and at any concentration. However, most ventilators on the market require medium pressure oxygen input (~150–350 kilopascals [kPa]) and fewer are designed to permit lower pressures typical from an oxygen concentrator (<55 kPa). Similarly, devices that use the Venturi effect to mix air or oxygen typically require medium pressure input to entrain air sufficiently.

Oxygen from a single outlet in the ward can be shared among multiple patients. In low-resource settings, this is often done informally by creating tube "trees" or "spiders" connecting multiple oxygen cannulae, however, there is no reliable way to know how much oxygen is going to each patient. Better methods involve the use of flowmeter assemblies (or "flow splitters" as shown in the image on the right) that will allow individualized titration to each patient.

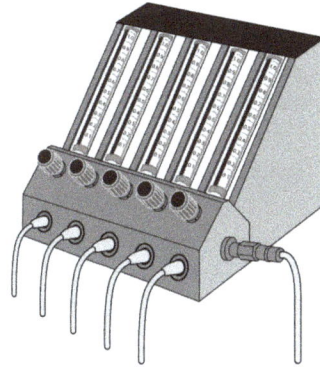

Figure 5: Oxygen Delivery Devices and Indicative Flow Rates and Inspired Oxygen Concentration

	Nasal prongs	Face mask	Reservoir mask	Venturi mask	High-flow nasal cannula	CPAP	Ventilator
	Low oxygen flow	Low oxygen flow	Moderate oxygen flow	Moderate oxygen flow (high mixed flow)	High oxygen flow	Variable oxygen flow (low to high)	Variable oxygen flow (low to high)
	For regular hospital and home care for most patients	For regular hospital and home care for most patients	For hospital care of more severely ill patients	For hospital care of more severely ill patients	For hospital care of critically ill patients	For hospital care of critically ill patients	For hospital care of critically ill patients
OXYGEN FLOW	0.1–5 liters/min	1–10 liters/min	10–15 liters/min	2–15 liters/min	10–70 liters/min	5–15 liters/min	5–30 liters/min
FiO_2 FRACTION INSPIRED OXYGEN	24%–50%	24%–50%	24%–50%	24%–60%	24%–60% (up to 100%)	24%–60% (up to 100%)	24%–60% (up to 100%)

CPAP = continuous positive airway pressure, FiO_2 = fraction of inspired oxygen, min = minute.
Note: Flow rates depend on size of patient (newborns much lower than adults), severity of illness, and specific type of device.
Source: Adapted by author from M. Hussein and A. Chughtai. 2021. How Is Medical Oxygen, Vital for COVID-19 Patients, Produced?. *Al Jazeera*. 11 May.: https://www.aljazeera.com/news/2021/5/11/covid-19-why-how-and-when-is-medical-oxygen-used.

Pulse Oximetry and the Health-Care Workforce

Health-care providers are currently a key limitation and opportunity for scaling-up oxygen for patients in LMICs. Nurses are typically the primary frontline users of oxygen therapy, responsible for screening patients for hypoxemia with pulse oximetry, initiating and adjusting oxygen therapy, and monitoring patients receiving oxygen support—although sometimes this role is prevented by restrictive scopes of practice. Other health-care workers, including doctors, medical assistants, nursing assistants, anesthetic technicians, and other paramedical health-care workers also use pulse oximetry and oxygen regularly.

Oxygen has similarities and unique differences from other essential medicines. Like all medicines, oxygen must be provided by skilled health-care workers who can provide the right amount of oxygen, to the right patient, at the right time. However, the administration of oxygen also requires health-care workers to have some specific knowledge about oxygen gas, delivery devices, and appropriate monitoring—particularly pulse oximetry. It also requires coordination with other health-care workers, technical and administrative staff regarding oxygen supply and use.

Oxygen and pulse oximetry are essential components of any acute care or respiratory illness training, and should be included in nursing, medical, and paramedical preservice teaching programs.[34] However, health-care worker surveys show that pulse oximetry and oxygen skills are not covered in existing preservice teaching programs or in-service training modules.[35] Upskilling of health-care workers, and provision of essential tools such as pulse oximetry, is essential to improve oxygen access globally (Case Study 2).

Pulse oximetry is the key clinical tool for guiding the use of oxygen. With much greater sensitivity and specificity for hypoxemia than clinical signs, pulse oximeters are now a global standard of care for hypoxemia management and regarded as a "priority medical device" by WHO.[36] Evidence from previous efforts to improve oxygen access show that adoption of pulse oximetry is the key driver in improved oxygen use and clinical effectiveness and more rational use.[37]

However, pulse oximetry is typically less widely used than oxygen, with multiple studies showing that <10% of acutely unwell patients are appropriately assessed with oximetry.[38] However, studies also show that pulse

---

[34] C. O. Schell et al. 2018. The Global Need for Essential Emergency and Critical Care. *Critical Care*. 22(1). p. 284. doi: 10.1186/s13054-018-2219-2 [published online first: 31 October 2018].

[35] A. S. Ginsburg et al. 2014. Oxygen and Pulse Oximetry in Childhood Pneumonia: Surveys of Clinicians and Student Clinicians in Cambodia. *Tropical Medicine and Internaltional Health*. 19(5). pp. 537–544. doi: 10.1111/tmi.12291; A. S. Ginsburg et al. 2012. Oxygen and Pulse Oximetry in Childhood Pneumonia: A Survey of Healthcare Providers in Resource-Limited Settings. *Journal of Tropical Pediatrics*. 58. pp. 389–393. doi: 10.1093/tropej/fmr103; A. A. Bakare et al. 2020. Providing Oxygen to Children and Newborns: A Multi-Faceted Technical and Clinical Assessment of Oxygen Access and Oxygen Use in Secondary-Level Hospitals in Southwest Nigeria. *International Health*. doi: 10.1093/inthealth/ihz009.

[36] WHO. 2020. *Priority Medical Devices List for the COVID-19 Response and Associated Technical Specifications: Interim Guidance*. 19 November. Geneva; WHO. 2016. *Interagency List of Priority Medical Devices for Essential Interventions for Reproductive, Maternal, Newborn and Child Health*. Geneva: WHO, UNICEF, UNFPA; L. Zhang et al. 2011. Accuracy of Symptoms and Signs in Predicting Hypoxaemia among Young Children with Acute Respiratory Infection: A Meta-Analysis [Review article]. *The International Journal of Tuberculosis and Lung Disease*. 15: pp. 317–325.

[37] H. R. Graham et al. 2019. Oxygen Systems to Improve Clinical Care and Outcomes for Children and Neonates: A Stepped-Wedge Cluster-Randomised Trial in Nigeria. *PLoS Medicine*. 16(11). e1002951. doi: https://doi.org/10.1371/journal.pmed.1002951.

[38] A. A. Bakare et al. 2020. Providing Oxygen to Children and Newborns: A Multi-Faceted Technical and Clinical Assessment of Oxygen Access and Oxygen Use in Secondary-Level Hospitals in Southwest Nigeria. *International Health*. doi: 10.1093/inthealth/ihz009; H. R. Graham et al. 2019. Oxygen Systems to Improve Clinical Care and Outcomes for Children and Neonates: A Stepped-Wedge Cluster-Randomised Trial in Nigeria. *PLoS Medicine*. 16(11). e1002951. doi: https://doi.org/10.1371/journal.pmed.1002951; R. K. Kayambankadzanja et al. 2021. Unmet Need of Essential Treatments for Critical Illness in Malawi. *PLoS ONE*. 16(9). e0256361. doi: 10.1371/journal.pone.0256361 [published online first: 11 September 2021].

oximetry can be introduced into routine care,[39] and embraced by health-care workers as "a tool that makes their work easier."[40] Rapid adoption of pulse oximetry and rational oxygen practices is possible,[41] but practice change is not immediate or automatic. For many health-care providers, pulse oximetry is a fundamentally new practice that requires coaching and support to become routine practice (footnote 41). Once health-care workers are familiar with pulse oximetry, they value it as "a tool that makes their work easier"—not just for detecting hypoxemia, but for assessment and monitoring of severely ill patients more broadly (footnote 40).

While pulse oximetry is widely valued as a diagnostic tool (identifying patients who warrant oxygen therapy), it is also an extremely valuable prognostic tool (identifying severely ill patients at high risk of death) and communication tool (between health-care workers and caregivers and/or patients).[42] This makes oximetry useful even in settings where oxygen therapy is not readily available, helping health-care workers identify and prioritize severely ill patients and communicate the need for referral and treatment with patients and/or caregivers. For this reason, oximetry is increasingly promoted as the fourth "vital sign" to be recorded for every acutely unwell patient (alongside temperature, heart rate, and respiratory rate).

Pulse oximetry is also the key for more efficient and effective use of oxygen at scale. In hospitals with some oxygen supplies, pulse oximetry can substantially increase oxygen coverage for hypoxemic patients while decreasing unnecessary and excessive usage, thereby improving both effectiveness and efficiency of oxygen services.[43] Therefore, scale-up of oximetry is an essential component of any effort to improve oxygen systems.

Pulse oximeters range in size and cost depending on quality and functionality (Table 1). Oximeters should meet WHO technical specifications and regulatory standards (e.g., ISO) (footnote 11). However, low-quality oximeters that do not meet minimum specifications are widely available globally and particularly in LMICs.[44]

Handheld devices are typically the best choice for most use cases, combining portability with adequate functionality and affordability. Donor investments to improve oximeter performance, durability, and cost have resulted in multiple high-quality devices now being widely available for around $250 (e.g., Masimo Rad G, Lifebox/Acare). Fingertip devices have limited application as their size and design typically compromise their

---

39   H. R. Graham et al. 2018. Adoption of Paediatric and Neonatal Pulse Oximetry by 12 Hospitals in Nigeria: A Mixed-Methods Realist Evaluation. *BMJ Global Health*. 3. e000812. doi: 10.1136/bmjgh-2018-000812; A. J. Enoch et al. 2020. Variability in the Use of Pulse Oximeters with Children in Kenyan Hospitals: A Mixed-Methods Analysis. *PLoS Med*. 16(12). e1002987. doi: 10.1371/journal. pmed.1002987 [published online first: 1 January 2020]; E. D. McCollum et al. 2016. Pulse Oximetry for Children with Pneumonia Treated as Outpatients in Rural Malawi. *Bulletin of the World Health Organization*. (94). pp. 893–902. doi: 10.2471/BLT.16.173401.

40   H. R. Graham et al. 2018. Adoption of Paediatric and Neonatal Pulse Oximetry by 12 Hospitals in Nigeria: A Mixed-Methods Realist Evaluation. *BMJ Global Health*. 3. e000812. doi: 10.1136/bmjgh-2018-000812.

41   H. R. Graham et al. 2018. Adoption of Paediatric and Neonatal Pulse Oximetry by 12 Hospitals in Nigeria: A Mixed-Methods Realist Evaluation. *BMJ Global Health*. 3. e000812. doi: 10.1136/bmjgh-2018-000812; A. J. Enoch et al. 2020. Variability in the Use of Pulse Oximeters with Children in Kenyan Hospitals: A Mixed-Methods Analysis. *PLoS Medicine*. 16(12). e1002987. doi: 10.1371/journal. pmed.1002987 [published online first: 1 January 2020].

42   H. R. Graham et al. 2018. Adoption of Paediatric and Neonatal Pulse Oximetry by 12 Hospitals in Nigeria: A Mixed-Methods Realist Evaluation. *BMJ Global Health*. 3. e000812. doi: 10.1136/bmjgh-2018-000812; A. Chandna et al. 2021. Anticipating the Future: Prognostic Tools as a Complementary Strategy to Improve Care for Patients with Febrile Illnesses in Resource-Limited Settings. *BMJ Global Health*. 6(7). doi: 10.1136/bmjgh-2021-006057 [published online first: 1 August 2021]; C. King et al. 2018. Opportunities and Barriers in Paediatric Pulse Oximetry for Pneumonia in Low-Resource Clinical Settings: A Qualitative Evaluation from Malawi and Bangladesh. *BMJ Open*. 8. e019177. doi: 10.1136/.

43   H. R. Graham et al. 2019. Oxygen Systems to Improve Clinical Care and Outcomes for Children and Neonates: A Stepped-Wedge Cluster-Randomised Trial in Nigeria. *PLoS Medicine*. 6(11). e1002951. doi: https://doi.org/10.1371/journal.pmed.1002951; R. K. Kayambankadzanja et al. 2021. Unmet Need of Essential Treatments for Critical Illness in Malawi. *PLoS ONE*. 16(9). e0256361. doi: 10.1371/journal.pone.0256361 [published online first: 11 September 2021].

44   The Open Oximetry project was recently launched to transparently report function of pulse oximeters to better empower users and purchasers. https://openoximetry.org/oximeters/.

performance in sick patients, particularly for children.[45] Desktop and more integrated monitoring devices are desirable for higher acuity settings where continuous monitoring of SpO_2 alongside other parameters is desirable (e.g., intensive care units).

Pulse oximeters consist of a probe and a computer processor. High-quality oximeter algorithms adjust for skin tone and thickness, movement, and low perfusion states—all of which are important in clinical application. Oximeters are covered by existing device standards (e.g., ISO, ICE), and United Nations Children's Fund (UNICEF) and partners have developed additional specifications that include key desirables such as warranty periods, functionality, battery time, and cost.

Table 1: Pulse Oximeter Types and Use Cases

Fingertip	Handheld	Desktop
Heart rate, SpO_2 Spot check Low cost <$100 Portable, not for children	Heart rate, SpO_2 (+/- RR, Hb) Spot, continuous Low cost ~$100 to $300 Versatile	HR, SpO_2 (+/- RR, Hb, ECG) Spot, continuous Cost ~$500 to $3,000 High acuity monitoring

ECG = electrocardiograph, Hb = hemoglobin, HR = heart rate, RR = respiratory rate, SpO_2 = peripheral blood oxygen saturation.

Source: Images from UNICEF/L'IV Com Sàrl/Steiner.

45   M. S. Lipnick et al. 2016. The Accuracy of 6 Inexpensive Pulse Oximeters Not Cleared by the Food and Drug Administration: The Possible Global Public Health Implications. *Anesthesia & Analgesia*. 123(2). pp. 338–345. doi: 10.1213/ANE.0000000000001300.

CASE STUDY 2

Cambodia, Global – Oxygen and Pulse Oximetry Access to Health-Care Workers

In a national survey of doctors and medical assistants in Cambodia, less than 20% of respondents reported that oxygen and pulse oximetry were available in their workplace "all the time."[46] Clinicians reported lower access to pulse oximetry than to oxygen therapy, and access was particularly poor in smaller district hospitals. The vast majority (>90%) of respondents cited "lack of training" and "lack of policies or guidelines" as the leading barriers to use, with maintenance issues reported less commonly (28% to 76%) and resistance from staff or patients, or cost barriers, reported relatively rarely (<20%). Similar survey results from Cambodian nursing and medical students suggested that pulse oximetry and oxygen were now present in preservice training (>80% had received some training), however, less than 20% had access to pulse oximetry in the facilities where they undertook clinical placements (footnote 46).

Surveys and clinical practice audits from other countries in the Asia and Pacific and Africa regions show a common thread: oxygen access and knowledge is low and pulse oximetry access and knowledge is even lower.[47] However, studies also show that pulse oximetry can be introduced into routine care (footnote 39), and embraced by health-care workers as "a tool that makes their work easier"—not just for detecting hypoxemia, but for assessment and monitoring of severely ill patients more broadly (footnote 40). Practice change is not immediate or automatic. For many nurses, pulse oximetry is a fundamentally new practice that requires coaching and support to become routine practice (footnote 41). One study tested the effect of introducing pulse oximetry prior to improving oxygen supply systems finding that oxygen coverage to hypoxemic patients increased threefold even before oxygen supplies had been improved (footnote 37).

This case study illustrates the importance of building health-care worker capacity to use oxygen well— recognizing that pulse oximetry is a key driver for improved hypoxemia management, better monitoring of severely ill patients, and reduced mortality.

---

46 A. S. Ginsburg et al. 2012. Oxygen and Pulse Oximetry In Childhood Pneumonia: A Survey of Healthcare Providers in Resource-Limited Settings. *Journal of Tropical Pediatrics*. 58. pp. 389–393. doi: 10.1093/tropej/fmr103.

47 C. King et al. 2018. Opportunities and Barriers in Paediatric Pulse Oximetry for Pneumonia in Low-Resource Clinical Settings: A Qualitative Evaluation from Malawi and Bangladesh. *BMJ Open*. 8. e019177. doi: 10.1136/; M. S. Lipnick et al. 2016. The Accuracy of 6 Inexpensive Pulse Oximeters Not Cleared by the Food and Drug Administration: The Possible Global Public Health Implications. *Anesthesia & Analgesia*. 123(2). pp. 338–345. doi: 10.1213/ANE.0000000000001300.

5 Oxygen Production, Storage, and Distribution

Key Messages

✔ **Cryogenic fractional distillation** is a cost-efficient method of producing high-purity liquid oxygen at very large scale. Cryogenic air separation units (ASUs) require substantial up-front investment and have high ongoing technical, transport (liquid oxygen delivery), and resource requirements (energy and water). Oxygen produced cryogenically is >99% pure and its liquid form means that it requires depressurization to gaseous form prior to distribution within a facility (typically into a piped distribution system). Liquid oxygen is a good option where competitive markets exist (e.g., regions with strong extractive industry sector) and long-term, stable, high-volume contracts are possible. It has safety and logistics requirements for transport and use, requiring a high level of technical and organizational capacity.

✔ **Pressure swing adsorption (PSA) and vacuum swing adsorption (VSA)** enable the production of oxygen from ambient air at varying scales (medium to high). PSA and VSA plants produce oxygen at 90% to 96% purity and can directly supply pressurized piped systems or be used to fill cylinders. On-site PSA and VSA plants are a good option for medium-sized to large hospitals and can be used to supply smaller hospitals through a hub-and-spoke model. PSA and VSA plants have modest capital costs and have been a popular investment by hospitals and governments, however, running costs (high) are often forgotten or ignored. PSA and VSA plants have substantial energy and maintenance requirements and careful planning is needed to ensure they operate continuously at capacity.

✔ **Oxygen concentrators** use the same PSA technology as larger oxygen plants producing oxygen at 90% to 96% purity. Oxygen from concentrators is produced at low pressure and can be supplied direct to patients, used with ventilators or CPAP, or pressurized for storage. Concentrators are a good option for small facilities, remote medical use, and emergency response, with low capital costs and lead time. Concentrators need reliable power supply and routine maintenance.

✅ **Oxygen cylinders** are best suited as backup oxygen supply, transport, or for small facilities with low oxygen demand, and are commonly used in larger facilities as well. Oxygen cylinders can be filled from liquid oxygen evaporation units or PSA and VSA plants. Oxygen cylinders must be used with pressure regulators to provide oxygen at a safe and appropriate pressure and can supply directly to patients or be distributed via piped systems. Oxygen cylinders' costs are highly variable and sensitive to changes in supply and demand. Costs are minimized by coordinated distribution over small geographic distances.

Summary of Oxygen Supply Options

The production, storage, distribution, and delivery of oxygen to facilities, wards, and patients can seem complex. Figure 6 and Table 2 summarize the main oxygen sources and delivery pathways.

In brief, oxygen is produced by cryogenic air separation units (producing liquid oxygen) or by oxygen plants or oxygen concentrators using pressure (or vacuum) swing adsorption (PSA or VSA). Liquid oxygen requires specialized transport and depressurization before entering a facility's gas distribution network (or used to fill cylinders). PSA and VSA plants produce gaseous oxygen that can supply directly into piped distribution systems or be used to fill cylinders. Oxygen concentrators and oxygen cylinders can be used directly to patients.

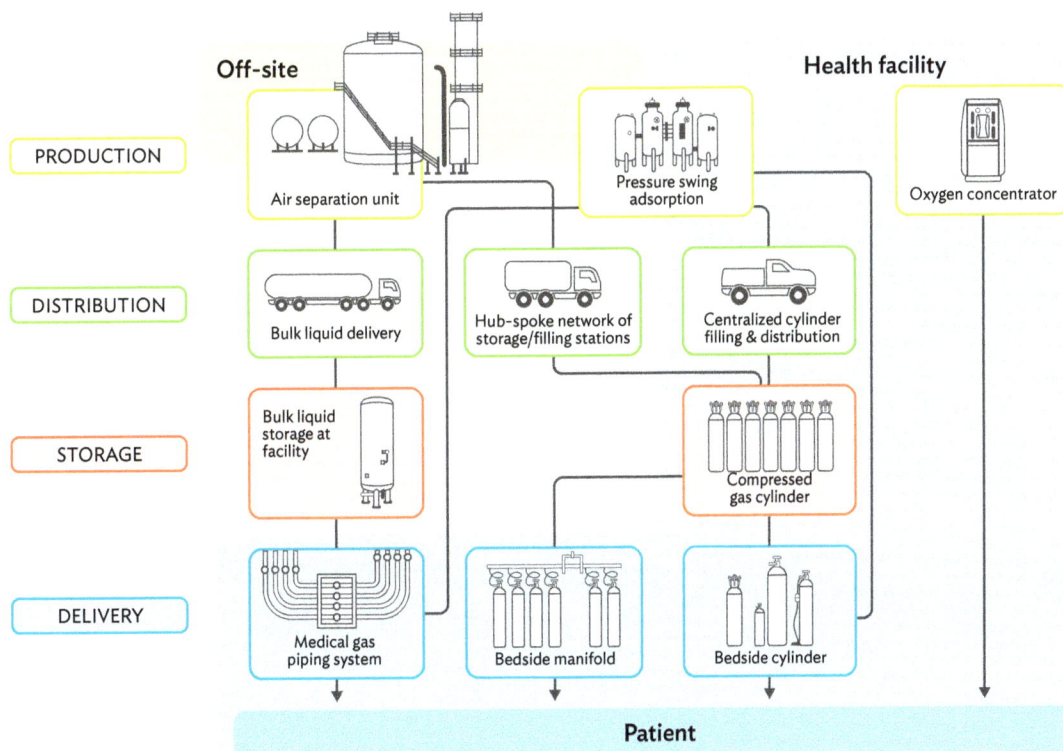

Figure 6: Pathways from Medical Oxygen Production to Distribution, Storage, and Clinical Use

Source: PATH, Clinton Health Access Initiative (CHAI). 2021. *Business Models in Respiratory Care*. Seattle: PATH, CHAI.

Table 2: Summary of the Main Medical Oxygen Supply Options to Facilities and Patients

	Cylinders	Concentrators	Oxygen plant (PSA or VSA)	Liquid Oxygen (ASU+VIE)
Description	A refillable metal storage vessel used to store and transport oxygen in compressed gas form. Cylinders require regular refilling at a gas plant and transportation to and from the plant.	A self-contained, electrically powered medical device designed to concentrate oxygen from ambient air, using PSA technology.	An on-site oxygen-generating system using PSA or VSA technology, supplying pressurized oxygen via a central pipeline system, or used to fill cylinders.	ASU produces high-volume liquid oxygen, stored and transported in bulk cryogenic tanks. VIEs store liquid oxygen on-site and convert to gas for use and require regular refilling.
Oxygen produced	Gas, high pressure. Oxygen purity depends on source (PSA versus cryogenic).	Gas, low pressure. Oxygen purity 90%–95%.	Gas, medium–high pressure. Oxygen purity 90%–95%.	Liquid, very high pressure. Oxygen purity 99%.
Use case	• Backup oxygen source. • Transport services. • Good primary oxygen source for small facilities, low demand. • Distribution in hub-and-spoke model from central plant. • Where power supply intermittent or unreliable.	• Good primary oxygen source for small facilities, low demand, and remote facilities with poor transport. • Home care.	• Direct supply to hospitals (medium-sized and large). • Central cylinder filling point in hub-and-spoke model.	• Direct supply to hospitals (medium-sized and large). • Central cylinder filling point for distribution. • Where power supply intermittent or unreliable.
Clinical application	For all oxygen needs, including high-pressure devices (CPAP, ventilators). Located nearby patient, or at central manifold for distribution to multiple patients and/or wards.	For most oxygen needs, except high-pressure devices (e.g., some CPAP machines and ventilators). Located nearby patients, for delivery direct or via flowmeter stand.	For all oxygen needs, including high-pressure supply (CPAP, ventilators). Located at central location on-site.	For all oxygen needs, including high-pressure supply and in facilities where power supply is intermittent or unreliable. VIE at central location on-site.

continued on next page

Table 2 continued

	Cylinders	Concentrators	Oxygen plant (PSA or VSA)	Liquid Oxygen (ASU+VIE)
Distribution mechanism	Connected to manifold of central or subcentral pipeline distribution system, or directly connected to patient with regulator, flowmeter, and tubing.	Direct to patient with tubing or to multiple patients via a flowmeter stand.	Central or subcentral pipeline distribution system, or can be used to refill cylinders (for distribution to manifold system, individual wards, or other facilities.	Central pipeline distribution system.
Electricity requirement	No	Yes	Yes	Minimal[a]
Maintenance requirement	Limited maintenance required by trained technicians.	Moderate maintenance required by trained technicians, who could be in-house.	Significant maintenance of system and piping required by highly trained technicians and engineers, can be provided as part of contract.	Significant maintenance of system and piping required by highly trained technicians and engineers, can be provided as part of contract.
User care	Moderate; regular checks of fittings and connections, regular checks of oxygen levels, cleaning exterior.	Moderate; cleaning of filters and device exterior.	Minimal; at terminal unit only.	Minimal; at terminal unit only.
Merits	• No power requirement. • Pressurized supply compatible with all devices. • Portable.	• Continuous oxygen supply (if power available). • Low up-front and running cost. • Output flow can be split among multiple patients.	• Continuous oxygen supply. • Can be cost-effective for large facilities. • Pressurized supply compatible with all devices.	• Minimal power requirements. • High-volume storage with small space requirement. • Pressurized supply compatible with all devices.
Drawbacks	• Exhaustible supply, small volume. • Requires transport and supply chain. • Highly reliant upon supplier. • Risk of gas leakage. • Risk of unwanted relocation. • Price highly variable and high running costs (refill, transport).	• Low-volume output (limited to one or few patients per device). • Low-pressure output (not suitable for many CPAP or ventilator devices). • Requires uninterrupted power. • Requires backup cylinder supply. • Requires maintenance.	• High capital investment and substantial running costs. • Requires uninterrupted power. • Needs adequate infrastructure. • High maintenance for piping. • Requires backup cylinder supply. • Risk of gas leakage from piping system.	• Requires transport and supply chain. • Exhaustible supply. • High maintenance for piping. • Needs adequate infrastructure. • Requires backup cylinder supply. • Risk of gas leakage from piping system.

ASU = air separation unit, PSA = pressure swing adsorption, VIE = vacuum-insulated evaporator, VSA = vacuum-swing adsorption.

[a] VIEs can supply central piped systems without requiring electricity to compress the gas, but they do need some power for alarm and safety systems (and additional power to fill cylinders); ASUs are huge gas production complexes with very high energy needs.

Source: World Health Organization. 2020. *Oxygen Sources and Distribution for COVID-19 Treatment Centres: Interim Guidance.* 4 April. Geneva. Images from UNICEF/L'IV Com Sàrl/Steiner.

Oxygen Production

Oxygen is produced by (i) cryogenic air separation units (ASUs) using **fractional distillation,** or (ii) oxygen plants of various sizes and bedside oxygen concentrators using **pressure or vacuum swing adsorption** (PSA or VSA).

Cryogenic Air Separation Units

Cryogenic fractional distillation is an energy-intensive process that involves liquefying air then separating the individual gases (nitrogen, oxygen, and others) at their respective boiling temperatures. The complexity and cost of fractional distillation means that ASUs are primarily used for producing compressed gas at a very large scale. For this reason, ASUs are often located in places with active mining and steel industries which use large quantities of compressed gas (nitrogen and oxygen) for extractive and production activities. Less commonly, smaller ASUs are deployed specifically for medical oxygen production.

Cryogenic fractional distillation can produce oxygen gas with **purity of 99.5% or higher**, and are governed by standards for Oxygen 99%.[48] Oxygen produced for medical use is essentially the same as oxygen produced for industrial use, but requires additional certification and regulatory oversight—both at the site of production and for the liquid oxygen tanks and vehicles used for transport and storage.[49]

ASUs are **typically privately owned by major gas companies** that serve heavy industry, especially the mining and steel industries. Establishing an ASU represents a very substantial investment, and requires robust construction oversight and strong understanding of gas safety and technical regulations. Advice from industry suggests that ASU commissioning typically takes at least 18 to 24 months from initiation with capital costs of $25 million for a 200 metric ton[50] per day plant to $125 million for a 3,000 ton per day plant (footnote 13).

Running ASUs requires highly skilled gas technicians and good safety and technical oversight to keep units running continuously 24/7. Major maintenance requires shutdown of the unit and may disrupt the supply chain substantially. ASUs have substantial running costs with particularly **high energy requirements** to achieve the necessary pressure/temperature, and **high water requirements** to keep compressors cool during the process. Over the life of an ASU, energy costs account for about 75% of total costs.

Given the large up-front and running costs, liquid gas producers need **clear and sustained demand** that closely matches their output capacity (not only of oxygen, but also of nitrogen to justify investment). To achieve this, producers typically rely on large, long-term contracts with industrial gas users and health facilities or sectors, with economic return and competitiveness of pricing highly dependent on maintaining high, steady demand, and optimizing energy efficiency. Transportation is the other major cost that can disadvantage facilities far away from an ASU. ASUs can typically serve customers within a 200–250 kilometer radius of the plant.

---

48   Council of Europe, European Pharmacopoeia Commission, and European Directorate for the Quality of Medicines & Healthcare. 2019. *European Pharmacopoeia.* 10th ed. Council of Europe; WHO. 2021. Medicinal Oxygen (Oxygenium Medicinalis): Draft proposal for revision in The International Pharmacopoeia (July 2021). Working document QAS/20867/Rev2. Geneva, Switzerland: WHO.

49   Medical oxygen has to be tested for oxygen purity, as well as the composition of remaining "impurities," with provision of a certificate of analysis ("C of A") to the purchaser. Facilities manufacturing medical oxygen must comply with the Pharmaceutical Inspection Co-operation Scheme (PIC/s) or WHO current good manufacturing practices (WHO cGMP). The chain of custody of bulk tanks and cylinders must be maintained throughout production and distribution (i.e., cylinders used solely for medical oxygen) to prevent contamination.

50   Two hundred metric tons of oxygen is equivalent to 175,000 liters of liquid oxygen or 140,000 normal cubic meter (Nm³) (140 million liters) of oxygen gas; 3,000 metric tons of oxygen is equivalent to 2.6 million liters of liquid oxygen or 2.1 million Nm³ (2,100 liters) of oxygen gas.

Oxygen produced by cryogenic fractional distillation must be **depressurized to gas** before it can be used to fill oxygen cylinders or enter a piped distribution system. Depressurizing can be done at the site of the ASU or the oxygen can be distributed to health facilities in liquid form using vacuum-insulated storage tanks to transport (on trucks) and store liquid oxygen at the facility. Typically, the cryogenic storage tanks and vaporizer remain the property and responsibility of the gas company producing the liquid oxygen, even if they are located on-site at a health facility, and the recipient takes ownership and responsibility for the oxygen after it is delivered in gaseous form.

There is **little competition in the liquid oxygen market**, with three companies dominating supply globally: the Linde Group (with regional subsidiaries including Afrox, BOC, Praxair, Inox), Air Liquide, and Air Products.[51] Other medical gas companies include the Taiyo Nippon Sanso Corporation and its subsidiaries, Air Water and Nippon Gases, the SOL Group, Messer, and Gulf Cryo. While countries such as the People's Republic of China and India have multiple companies producing and supplying liquid oxygen, many smaller and island countries in the Asia and Pacific region have no, or minimal, access. Unitaid and CHAI have negotiated in principal agreements with Air Liquide and the Linde Group to expand access to liquid oxygen and are in discussions with other companies.[52]

Medical oxygen is a small fraction of the liquid gas market and the location of ASUs is usually determined by industrial demand. ASUs are often established alongside a particular industry client as part of a multibillion-dollar agreement providing the client with reliable gas supply and giving the gas company security to make such a large investment. A single ASU may produce sufficient liquid oxygen to supply the medical needs of entire provinces or even multiple small countries, but the logistics of distributing liquid oxygen are complex.

Suppliers often charge a premium for "medical" versus "industrial" oxygen, however the additional actual costs are minimal when providing oxygen at scale. Investigative reporting has revealed irregularities and variation in how pricing is applied to the health sector.[53]

Use Case, Challenges, and Opportunities
ASUs produce very high volumes of oxygen (and nitrogen) in high-pressure liquid form, primarily for industrial users. A single ASU can produce enough oxygen for an entire province or small country. Liquid oxygen is efficient to transport and can be supplied at health facilities without substantial energy inputs, but does come with additional safety considerations and logistics requirements. This makes liquid oxygen an excellent source of bulk oxygen for small and large facilities, both through direct delivery into piped hospital oxygen systems and filling cylinders for distribution.

The biggest challenges for liquid oxygen-based systems are as follows:
(i) **Geographic access.** ASUs are typically located in major industrial areas and some countries have no ASUs providing medical oxygen in country. Liquid oxygen can be efficiently transported where road or rail access is reasonable—and even across international borders and by sea—but it does entail additional cost and logistics complexity.

51 WHO. 2021. *WHO Technical Consultation on Oxygen Access Scale-Up for COVID-19*. Geneva.
52 Unitaid. 2021. Unprecedented Cooperation with Global Oxygen Suppliers Paves Way to Increase Access for Low- and Middle-Income Countries to Address COVID-19 Crisis. 15 June. https://unitaid.org/news-blog/unprecedented-cooperation-global-oxygen-suppliers-june-2021/#en.
53 M. Davies, L. Rios, and C. Giles. 2021. Oxygen Firms Accused of Intimidating Mexican Hospitals During Pandemic. *The Guardian*; M. Davies, A. Onwuzoo, and S. Mednick. 2020. Fighting for Breath: How the Medical Oxygen Industry is Failing African Hospitals. *The Guardian*. 10 August.

(ii) **Low health sector leveraging power and high cost**. Liquid medical oxygen contract conditions for health facilities are typically much poorer than for large-scale industrial users, particularly when contracts are negotiated for small groups of facilities (low volume) over short periods of time with limited financial commitment from the health sector. Therefore, liquid oxygen supplies are typically expensive.

(iii) **Gas sector capital investment risk**. ASUs are typically built after securing a major financial commitment from a core customer, typically a major industrial company. Investment in an ASU primarily for medical oxygen purposes would be regarded as risky.

(iv) **Safety requirements**. ASU plants require a high level of technical staffing and safety requirements. Associated liquid oxygen infrastructure at facilities is less cumbersome, but still has stringent base technical and safety requirements.

There is substantial opportunity for improving access to liquid oxygen via the major gas companies and smaller distributors.

(i) **Large contracts**. The cost of liquid oxygen supply to facilities can be substantially reduced through pooled negotiation across entire provinces (or even countries).

(ii) **De-risk liquid oxygen supply to health sector**. In addition to negotiated contracts, there may be opportunity for other financial and business mechanisms to help reduce the risks for liquid oxygen producers and distributors, e.g., secured contracts.

(iii) **Increase competition**. The liquid oxygen market has little competition and could respond positively if additional major oxygen suppliers (liquid or using PSA or VSA plants) entered the market.

(iv) **Stimulate distributors**. Small and medium-sized enterprises are already functioning as distributors in many markets, aggregating demand and coordinating supply. This is an opportunity to encourage efficiency and competition, particularly for those serving harder-to-reach areas.

Pressure Swing Adsorption and Vacuum Swing Adsorption Oxygen Plants

Pressure swing adsorption (PSA) is an energy-intensive process that compresses ambient air and passes it through a sieve bed to remove nitrogen. The sieve bed typically contains zeolite—a porous mineral that allows oxygen molecules to pass through—but traps the larger nitrogen molecules. Trapped nitrogen is then flushed out from the zeolite using an alternating pressure cycle, refreshing the zeolite to trap nitrogen again in the next cycle.

Vacuum swing adsorption (VSA) uses a similar process, but uses a vacuum blower instead of an air compressor to draw ambient air through the sieve bed and produce oxygen. VSA plants typically require higher capital investment than a comparable PSA plant, but are more energy-efficient, have lower operating costs, and can operate at higher altitudes without a reduction in performance (footnote 13).

PSA or VSA produces oxygen gas with **purity of 90% to 96%** (the remainder mostly argon), although newer technology can also remove argon and achieve purity of 96% to 99%. This is governed under the gas standards for Oxygen 93% (footnotes 20 and 22) and is described in the relevant WHO technical specifications for PSA plants (footnote 29). This is governed under the gas standards for Oxygen 93 (footnote 48) and is described in the relevant WHO technical specifications for PSA plants (footnote 31).

The oxygen produced from PSA or VSA plants can provide oxygen directly **into a pressurized piped** oxygen system (with appropriate safety precautions) and/or be compressed further to **fill oxygen cylinders** ("filling stations").[54]

---

54   VSA plants have lower output pressure than PSA plants, so they may need a compressor to feed into a piped distribution system.

PSA or VSA plants may be privately or publicly owned and may be located on-site at a major hospital or at a separate industrial complex. They can vary greatly in capacity, from under 50 liters per minute (LPM) to over 2,500 LPM (~5,000 SCFH, ~140 normal cubic meter [Nm^3] per hour).[55] Production and shipping time can be 4–36 weeks, depending on supplier capacity, size, customization, and distance. Installation is technically and logistically complex and requires technicians who can assemble components on-site and run safety tests. Some smaller plants may be pre-assembled, for example, in a shipping container, or premounted on a steel skid ("skid mounted"), which does add costs, but reduces time and potential issues during installation.

Capital cost depends on capacity, functionality (e.g., filling station), regulatory requirements, and the supply of accessories, spare parts, and infrastructure improvements. Indicative capital costs for a large hospital (1,000+ beds) requiring 120 Nm^3 per hour may be $500,000–$800,000 for a PSA plant and 10% more expensive for a VSA plant (footnote 13).

Running costs are driven by high energy requirements, technical personnel, and maintenance. Indicative running costs for a 2,880 Nm^3 per day PSA plant is approximately $1,990 per month, and $1,000 for a VSA plant (footnote 13).

Preventive and corrective maintenance is essential and requires skilled technicians. These services may be provided under a contractor agreement with suppliers, but access to local technical expertise and spare parts is still required for prompt servicing. Maintenance challenges relate to operation in heat and humidity, requiring regular attention to filters, lubricants, calibrating pressures, and purity of oxygen production—and reliable access to spare parts (which are often imported). Failure of valves, compressors, or sieve beds require shutdown of the unit and ready access to spare parts and technical support to prevent prolonged shutdown.

Return on investment is maximized when plants run at full capacity and variability in demand is controlled. This can be achieved by locating high-capacity oxygen plants at major hospitals and distributing excess oxygen to smaller facilities, particularly if production and distribution can be pooled across many facilities (i.e., overlapping hub-and-spoke model). However, this model does incur additional costs in logistics personnel and transport as well as added energy and maintenance costs for the filling station.

Use Case, Challenges, and Opportunities

PSA and VSA plants enable continuous production of moderate to high volume oxygen on-site (or off-site) and can be deployed relatively quickly and at modest cost. This makes them useful for supplying major hospitals, particularly where liquid oxygen is not available or too expensive, and for using as the central hub to fill and distribute cylinders to smaller facilities (hub-and-spoke model, Case Study 3).

The biggest challenges for PSA and VSA-based systems are as follows:
  (i) **Inadequate design.** Design of a PSA or VSA plant must match the intended use, including capacity to meet increased demand over time and appropriateness to local staffing and infrastructure capacity. Additional features may be needed for particular use cases, such as filling station to fill cylinders for onward distribution. Technical specifications exist, but are often not applied (footnote 31).
  (ii) **Requirement for reliable power**. Depending on size, the power draw from a PSA or VSA plant may be greater than the combined power needed for all other hospital services and often require a significant power upgrade. Poor quality power supply will damage compressors and accelerate failure.

---

55   Standard cubic foot gas measured at 1 atmosphere and 70°F. Normal cubic meter (Nm^3) gas measured at 1 atmosphere and 0°C. Liters per minute (LPM) gas measured at 1 atmosphere and 20°C.

(iii) **Equipment failure due to inadequate maintenance and lack of spare parts**. PSA and VSA plants require 24/7 technician availability and regular maintenance by technical experts to prevent and address small problems before they lead to complete failure. Reliable access to spare parts is essential and many will need to be imported.

(iv) **Inefficient operation and distribution**. Inadequate staffing and erratic power supply can result in PSA or VSA plants running well under capacity and failing to deliver efficient returns on investment. Similarly, in hub-and-spoke models, inadequate supply of cylinders and weak delivery systems can prevent the oxygen produced from reaching patients in smaller facilities.

There is substantial opportunity for improving and scaling PSA and VSA plant technology and business models and integrating with other health systems and infrastructure programs (especially power).

(i) **Expand access to PSA and VSA plants**. Many manufacturers of PSA and VSA plants, and sources of components, are in the Asia region. There is opportunity to expand the reach and scope of services of existing small and medium-sized enterprises by helping them carry financial risk and capital (e.g., leasing agreements).

(ii) **Better maintenance and supply models**. Sustainability should be a major focus of PSA-based oxygen programs; particularly establishing business models that promote effective, timely preventive maintenance in broad geographic areas. Increasing emphasis is being placed on oxygen supply as a service, rather than oxygen devices as procured equipment. There is opportunity to stimulate oxygen service providers to operate between manufacturers and health facilities (Case Study 4).

(iii) **Integration with improved power**. PSA and VSA plants need power, and power providers need reliable demand. There is opportunity to invest in improved rural power supply projects alongside PSA or VSA plants as a core customer (e.g., solar-powered microgrids).

(iv) **Integration with health infrastructure**. PSA and VSA plants require certain personnel, systems, and infrastructure that also benefit other aspects of health facility capacity and function. There is opportunity to build biomedical and infrastructure capacity of facilities alongside PSA or VSA plant development.

CASE STUDY 3

Kenya – Hub-and-Spoke Model of Oxygen Supply

Hewatele is a social enterprise that operates an oxygen supply service using pressure swing adsorption (PSA) plants based at major hospitals combined with a hub-and-spoke distribution model to supply oxygen cylinders to smaller facilities. This model was developed from a collaboration between the nonprofit Center for Public Health and Development, funder (GE Foundation), technical partner (Assist International and Frog Design), and district hospital authority. As a social enterprise, Hewatele aims to maximize affordability and equity, rather than profit. Its privatized structure seeks to aggregate the costs and logistical requirements across multiple facilities and present a low-risk oxygen supply solution to government. Government facilities have benefited from more affordable and reliable oxygen supplies. Hewatele is currently planning to build a liquid oxygen plant (air separation unit) to increase supply as it has been unable to meet the high demand. However, an ongoing challenge is to make this model financially independent of donor support.

continued on next page

Case Sudy 3 continued

This case study illustrates the use of PSA plant hub-and-spoke models to expand oxygen distribution geographically. To address financial viability, the Institute for Transformative Technologies launched the **Oxygen Hub**[56] with funders Skoll Foundation and ELMA Philanthropies—a franchise model that supports local entrepreneurs to establish PSA oxygen businesses through negotiated equipment, blended financing, and management support. To date, PSA plants have been opened in Nigeria (managed by Airbank), Kenya (managed by TopCare), and Ethiopia (managed by KeaMed) with more launches planned. Oxygen Hub is still young, but illustrates the kind of innovative financing that is required to expand oxygen access and build sustainable oxygen systems.

Hewatele Oxygen Plant. Medical oxygen cylinders on a truck at the Hewatele Oxygen Plant in Kenya (photo by Thomas Mukoya/Reuters).

56   Oxygen Hub. https://oxygenhub.org/.

Malawi – Invest in Maintenance

Adequate maintenance personnel, procedures, and spare parts can extend equipment life span, optimize oxygen supply, and maximize return on capital investment. During the coronavirus disease (COVID-19) pandemic in 2021, technicians in Malawi showed how maintenance and repair of existing oxygen concentrators and pressure swing adsorption (PSA) plants could quickly increase oxygen supply.

Build Health International (BHI) estimates that around half of PSA plants installed in LMIC in the past 15 years are not functioning at all or are operating well under capacity. In 2021, BHI assessed the function of seven PSA oxygen plants in Malawi, finding that three plants were nonfunctional due to major electrical issues, failed filters, or major safety failures. Of the four plants that were at least partially functional, performance was compromised by lack of spare parts or tools, lack of technicians to staff the plant 24/7, and low-quality components that needed replacement. However, even the nonfunctional plants could be repaired at a cost of $5,000 to $25,000, approximately one-tenth the cost of a new equivalent plant and could be repaired much more quickly. Repairing these plants would increase oxygen supply by 600 cubic meters per day serving up to 800 adults or 2,000 children with oxygen continuously.

The **OpenO2** team has done similar repair work for oxygen concentrators, fitting out minivans as mobile oxygen repair units and traveling to hospitals throughout the country to revive broken oxygen concentrators. As of October 2021, the team had repaired 649 oxygen concentrators for a total cost of $97,000, a fraction of the cost of replacing them with new concentrators and could be repaired much more quickly. These repaired concentrators have the combined capacity to treat up to 4,607 adults or 34,553 babies with a continuous flow of oxygen for 1 week.

Concentrator repair. Before and after photographs of concentrators (photo by OpenO2).

Oxygen Concentrators

Oxygen concentrators use the same **pressure swing adsorption** technology as PSA plants, but at smaller scale (typically 5-10 LPM). Concentrators are commercially available as medical devices and included on the interagency list of priority medical devices and UNICEF supply catalog.[57]

---

[57]   WHO. 2016. *Interagency List of Priority Medical Devices for Essential Interventions for Reproductive, Maternal, Newborn and Child Health.* Geneva, Switzerland: WHO, UNICEF, and UNFPA..

Oxygen concentrators produce oxygen gas with **purity of 90% to 96%** (the remainder, mostly argon), meeting the gas standards for Oxygen 93 (footnotes 20 and 22). Additional requirements are described more fully in the WHO technical specifications for oxygen concentrators.[58]

The oxygen produced from oxygen concentrators is at **lower pressure** and can be directly administered to patients or distributed within a ward using flow-splitter devices and low-pressure tubing. Concentrators can also be used alongside some ventilators and continuous positive airway pressure (CPAP) machines, or used to fill low-, medium-, or high-pressure storage vessels (high-pressure storage vessels requiring additional compression via a mobile filling station).

Oxygen concentrators are typically purchased from **medical device suppliers** with a short warranty period (typically 1 year). They should have approval from a regulatory authority (e.g., Food and Drug Administration [FDA], CE mark) and meet the most current International Organization for Standardization (ISO) 800601-2-69 standard. However, there are hundreds of concentrators on the market and are present in health facilities that do not meet any of these standards.[59]

Production time is typically short (~2 weeks), but has exceeded 8–12 weeks during COVID-19 high demand, with additional 2–12 weeks for shipping depending on distance and local clearance. Installation is simple, and basic flow-splitting and low-pressure distribution systems can be done by trained local technicians. Speed and simplicity of deployment makes concentrator-based systems a preferred option for emergency response and they featured strongly in COVID-19 response to serve the bulk of hospitalized cases who required lower flows.[60]

Capital cost of concentrators depends on size, quality of components, functionality and safety inclusions (e.g., oxygen purity alarm), regulatory approvals, the supply of accessories, spare parts, and whether infrastructure improvements are required (e.g., shelter, power supply). A single 5 LPM concentrator may cost between $400 and $2,000 (excluding spare parts or maintenance contract), and larger capacity concentrators may be much more expensive.

Oxygen analyzers are essential devices for all facilities with oxygen systems and are particularly important for concentrator-based systems in which local technicians have the primary responsibility for device management. Built-in oxygen purity alarms are a requirement for concentrators under the ISO 80601-2-69 standard, but many concentrators are supplied without one. Oxygen analyzers cost $80–$400 and may also measure pressure or other parameters.

Running costs are driven by power requirements and costs of repairs and maintenance (which can be minimized with regular cleaning and care). Concentrators are vulnerable to low-quality power supply, as voltage fluctuations damage the compressor. Renewable energy is increasingly seen as an option for concentrators and may be similar

58   WHO. 2013. *Pocket Book of Hospital Care for Children: Guidelines for the Management of Common Childhood Illnesses.* 2nd ed. Geneva.
59   A. A. Bakare et al. 2020. Providing Oxygen to Children and Newborns: A Multi-Faceted Technical and Clinical Assessment of Oxygen Access and Oxygen Use in Secondary-Level Hospitals in Southwest Nigeria. *International Health.* doi: 10.1093/inthealth/ihz009; H. R. Graham et al. 2021. Measuring Oxygen Access: Lessons from Health Facility Assessments in Lagos, Nigeria. *BMJ Global Health.* 6(8). doi: 10.1136/bmjgh-2021-006069; Open O2. 2021. *Open O2 Hub for Innovation and Information in Oxygen Concentration Technology.* Lilongwe, Malawi: Global Health Informatics Institute. https://www.openo2.org (accessed 1 September 2021).
60   WHO. 2020. *Oxygen Sources and Distribution for COVID-19 Treatment Centres.* Geneva; WHO. 2020. *Coronavirus Disease (COVID-19) Technical Guidance: Essential Resource Planning.* Geneva. https://www.who.int/emergencies/diseases/novel-coronavirus-2019/technical-guidance/covid-19-critical-items (accessed 16 April 2020).

in cost to the use of gasoline or diesel generators over their life span,[61] but whole-of-facility energy solutions, if feasible, are likely to be best.

Preventive and corrective maintenance is essential and can be performed by trained health-care workers and technicians. Most concentrators are designed for in-home use for European and North American markets and do not perform optimally in hot, humid, or dusty conditions. Common causes of device failure can be largely prevented by regular cleaning and replacement of filters and avoiding forcing the device beyond its recommended capacity. Trained staff can do simple fixes for broken internal tubing, valve malfunction, and similar, if spare parts are available. Additional technical expertise may be required for refurbishment or replacement of compressors, sieve beds, or circuit boards.

Return on investment is maximized when concentrators are maintained well. Typically, the amount of oxygen supplied to patients is less than the concentrator capacity (concentrators must run continuously whether the patient needs are 1 LPM or 5 LPM), hence, the addition of local storage may increase energy- and cost-efficiency further.

Use Case, Challenges, and Opportunities

Oxygen concentrators enable continuous production of oxygen on-site at low volume and can be deployed relatively quickly and at low cost. This makes them useful for emergency response and deployment in small and remote health facilities (and homes).

The biggest challenges for concentrator-based systems are the following:

(i)   **Requirement for reliable power**. Poor-quality power supply will damage compressors and accelerate failure, and power cuts can interrupt oxygen supply, putting lives at risk. So many oxygen concentrator projects also require improved power. Oxygen concentrators have been successfully combined with solar power,[62] and cost-effectiveness can be very favorable despite the substantially higher capital costs.

---

61   H. R. Graham et al. 2019. Oxygen Systems to Improve Clinical Care and Outcomes for Children and Neonates: A Stepped-Wedge Cluster-Randomised Trial in Nigeria. *PLoS Medicine*. 16(11). e1002951. doi: https://doi.org/10.1371/journal.pmed.1002951; Y. Huang et al. 2021. Estimated Cost-Effectiveness of Solar-Powered Oxygen Delivery for Pneumonia in Young Children in Low-Resource Settings. *JAMA Netw Open*. 4(6). e2114686. doi: 10.1001/jamanetworkopen.2021.14686 [published online first: 25 June 2021]; S. R. Howie et al. 2020. The Development and Implementation of an Oxygen Treatment Solution for Health Facilities in Low and Middle-Income Countries. *Journal of Global Health*. 10(2). p. 020425. doi: 10.7189/jgh.10.020425 [published online first: 5 December 2020]; T. Duke et al. 2020. Solar-Powered Oxygen, Quality Improvement and Child Pneumonia Deaths: A Large-Scale Effectiveness Study. *Archives of Disease in Childhood*. doi: 10.1136/archdischild-2020-320107 [published online first: 18 October 2020]; Q. Mian et al. 2019. Solar-Powered Oxygen Delivery to Treat Childhood Pneumonia in Low-Resource Settings: A Randomised Controlled Non-Inferiority Trial and Cost-Effectiveness Study. *The Lancet Global Health*. 7. doi: 10.1016/s2214-109x(19)30095-6; T. Duke et al. 2016. Solar Powered Health Care. *International Journal of Tuberculosis and Lung Disease*. 20(5). pp. 572–573. doi: 10.5588/ijtld.16.0210; H. Turnbull et al. 2016. Solar-Powered Oxygen Delivery: Proof of Concept. *International Journal of Tuberculosis and Lung Disease*. 20(5). pp. 696–703. doi: 10.5588/ijtld.15.0796.

62   Y. Huang et al. 2021. Estimated Cost-Effectiveness of Solar-Powered Oxygen Delivery for Pneumonia in Young Children in Low-Resource Settings. *JAMA Netw Open*. 4(6). e2114686. doi: 10.1001/jamanetworkopen.2021.14686 [published online first: 25 June 2021]; S. R. Howie et al. 2020. The Development and Implementation of an Oxygen Treatment Solution for Health Facilities in Low and Middle-Income Countries. *Journal of Global Health*. 10(2). 020425. doi: 10.7189/jgh.10.020425 [published online first: 5 December 2020]; T. Duke et al. 2016. Solar Powered Health Care. *International Journal of Tuberculosis and Lung Disease*. 20(5). pp. 572–573. doi: 10.5588/ijtld.16.0210; H. Turnbull et al. 2016. Solar-Powered Oxygen Delivery: Proof of Concept. *International Journal of Tuberculosis and Lung Disease*. 20(5). pp. 696–703. doi: 10.5588/ijtld.15.0796; T. Duke et al. 2017. Solar Powered Oxygen Systems in Remote Health Centers in Papua New Guinea: A Large Scale Implementation Effectiveness Trial. *Journal of Global Health*. 7(1).doi: 10.7189/jogh.07.010411; M. T. Hawkes et al. 2018. Solar-Powered Oxygen Delivery in Low-Resource Settings: A Randomized Clinical Noninferiority Trial. *JAMA Pediatrics*. E1-2. doi: 10.1001/jamapediatrics.2018.0228; J. A. Litch and R. A. Bishop. 2000. Oxygen Concentrators for the Delivery of Supplemental Oxygen in Remote High-Altitude Areas. *Wilderness & Environmental Medicine*. 11(3). pp. 189–191; B. Morrissey, N. Conroy, and A. Estelle. 2015. Effect of Solar Panels on In-Patient Paediatric Mortality in a District Hospital in Sierra Leone. *Archives of Disease in Childhood*. 100. A114. doi: http://dx.doi.org/10.1136/archdischild-2015-308599.253; S. Namasopo et al. 2014. Solar-Powered Oxygen Delivery. *American Journal of Tropical Medicine and Hygiene*. 1. p. 15; F. Pulsan and T. Duke. 2020. Response to Oxygen Therapy Using Oxygen Concentrators Run Off Solar Power in Children with Respiratory Distress in Remote Primary Health Facilities in Papua New Guinea. *Tropical Doctor*. 49475520947886. doi: 10.1177/0049475520947886 [published online first: 19 August 2020]; H. R. Graham et al. 2017. Improving Oxygen Therapy for Children and Neonates in Secondary Hospitals in Nigeria: Study Protocol for a Stepped-Wedge Cluster Randomised Trial. *Trials*. 18(1). p. 502. doi: 10.1186/s13063-017-2241-8.

(ii) **Equipment failure due to inadequate maintenance**. The presence of oxygen concentrators in hospital equipment "graveyards" is commonplace, particularly those donated from high-income countries.[63] Harsh environmental conditions, particularly heat and humidity, present challenges to devices that were originally designed for home use in temperate or air-conditioned climates. However, concentrators can function effectively for many years with low ongoing costs if they are regularly cleaned and maintained with access to spare parts and repair technical assistance, particularly if more reliable models are used.[64]

(iii) **Small volume supply**. Oxygen concentrators typically produce 5 LPM or 10 LPM of oxygen, which can be shared between multiple children on low-flow oxygen, but may not be sufficient for a single adult requiring higher flows. The low-pressure output of concentrators also limits its ability to interface with some types of ventilators. Thus, concentrators are less suitable as a primary oxygen solution for hospitals with high patient flow requirements or intensive care.

There is substantial opportunity for improving oxygen concentrator technology and supply and maintenance models.

(i) **Better concentrators**. Funders have supported oxygen concentrator technological innovation in recent years, resulting in more robust, easily maintained, and user-friendly concentrators approaching market entry. Additional innovation in functionality will further improve their appropriateness and efficiency, including linkage to oxygen storage, built-in power stabilization, and better energy efficiency. UNICEF's Oxygen Concentrator Innovation Project is working with partners to develop new target product profiles for oxygen concentrators and engage manufacturers, with an opportunity for funders to support more rapid technological innovation and market availability.

(ii) **Better maintenance and supply models**. Sustainability is now the focus of concentrator-based oxygen programs, establishing business models that promote effective maintenance even in remote areas. Oxygen partners are increasingly talking about oxygen supply as a service, rather than oxygen devices as procured equipment. There is an opportunity for funders to support the development and scale-up of more effective supply and maintenance business models for small and remote facilities.

CASE STUDY 5

Tonga – Oxygen for Remote Health Facilities

Tonga is a Pacific nation of 169 islands, with total land area of 700 square kilometers (km^2) spread across over 600,000 km^2 of ocean. Around 70% of the population of just over 100,000 live in the main island, Tongatapu. Prior to 2017, most oxygen in Tonga was supplied from a pressure swing adsorption plant in Tongatapu, and it was challenging to reliably produce and distribute oxygen in cylinders across the islands.

Niu'ui Hospital in the Ha'apai island group of Tonga had a significant oxygen requirement and experienced difficulties maintaining oxygen supplies without interruption; hence, power reliability was poor. In 2017, the Tonga Ministry of Health, partnering with CureKids NZ, the University of Auckland, and Azimut 360, installed several oxygen concentrators powered by a movable, plug-and-play solar trailer, providing reliable high-quality power.

Continued on next page

63   S. R. Howie et al. 2008. Beyond Good Intentions: Lessons on Equipment Donation from an African Hospital. *Bulletin of the World Health Organization*. 86(1). pp. 52–56.
64   B. D. Bradley et al. 2015. A Retrospective Analysis of Oxygen Concentrator Maintenance Needs and Costs in a Low-Resource Setting: Experience from The Gambia. *Health and Technology*. 4(4). pp. 319–328. doi: http://dx.doi.org/10.1007/s12553-015-0094-2.

Case Study 5 continued

Local clinical, biomedical, and electrical engineering staff were engaged and trained in hypoxemia detection, concentrators, and solar system use and maintenance, enhancing sustainability and local ownership. The system ensured 100% availability for hypoxemic patients, reduced cylinders use dramatically, and was rated by staff as easy to use. The solar system design took into account the risk of corrosion and exposure to cyclones, being easy to dismantle so that after a cyclone (e.g., Gita in 2016), power continues to be available at the hospital, not only for oxygen production, but for other essential medical needs.

Similar solar-powered, oxygen concentrator-based solutions have supported the expansion of oxygen to small health facilities in other remote areas.[65] A large program that introduced solar-powered oxygen to 30 small health facilities in remote **Papua New Guinea** found greater than 50% reduction in child pneumonia mortality at a cost of $6,435 per life saved and over 1,500 referrals avoided.[66]

These case studies demonstrate the usefulness of solar-powered oxygen concentrators in remote settings. However, they have also needed to overcome numerous challenges to ensure equipment is maintained, spare parts are available, and technical expertise is available when needed.

Remote oxygen facilities. Movable plug-and-play solar set-up with trailer in Tonga (photo by Azimut 360).

Oxygen Storage and Distribution

Different oxygen supply technologies will lend themselves to different models of oxygen distribution to facilities, and within facilities—and different maintenance approaches.

Liquid oxygen supply systems depend on centralized production and this may introduce limitations on the scope of geographic distribution as it depends on specialized liquid gas tankers. Where it is cost-effective to deliver liquid oxygen in bulk, there are options for supplying facilities directly (on-site vacuum-insulated evaporator [VIE]) and/or filling oxygen cylinders for further distribution to smaller facilities (with associated transport

---

65   T. Duke et al. 2016. Solar Powered Health Care. *International Journal of Tuberculosis and Lung Disease.* 20(5). pp. 572–573. doi: 10.5588/ijtld.16.0210.

66   T. Duke et al. 2020. Solar-Powered Oxygen, Quality Improvement and Child Pneumonia Deaths: A Large-Scale Effectiveness Study. *Archives of Disease in Childhood.* doi: 10.1136/archdischild-2020-320107 [published online first: 18 October 2020].

costs). Liquid oxygen supply systems require centralized maintenance programs to manage everything, but the day-to-day function of VIEs.

PSA and VSA plants enable localized production of oxygen and can be used to supply facilities directly and/or fill cylinders. While the transport of gaseous oxygen in cylinders is simpler than liquid oxygen, it still requires substantial logistics to fill cylinders and distribute to facilities—particularly in more remote or isolated areas—and the transport costs can be high. Maintenance models for PSA- and VSA-based distribution systems can vary from entirely decentralized to largely centralized, although plants will always require some technical capacity on-site.

Concentrators are a very localized oxygen production solution that can be distributed to a small number of patients, but will not fit with a pressurized piped oxygen hospital distribution system. Maintenance models for concentrator-based distribution systems can be decentralized, but are much more reliable and efficient if there is some centralization of repair and spare parts.

Bulk Liquid Oxygen Storage Tanks and Vacuum-Insulated Evaporator

Liquid oxygen is stored and transported in cryogenic tanks made up of **double-layered steel** with an insulating vacuum space in between. Storage tanks range in size, typically containing 500–25,000 liters of liquid oxygen[67] at 18–36 bar of pressure.

Facilities that use liquid oxygen will have a **VIE** on-site, consisting of the storage tank, vaporizers, valves, piping, and pressure control system. VIEs must be in a secure outdoor area, accessible to a tanker for refill, and away from potential fire sources (e.g., diesel generators).

The VIE **depressurizes the liquid oxygen** to gaseous oxygen and controls the pressure, releasing flows of 150–20,000 liters of gas per minute depending on design. The vaporizer must be an appropriate size for the facility and ventilated to prevent excessive icing[68] (usually multiple vaporizers are installed and operate cyclically).

VIEs typically supply oxygen directly into a **piped system**. The most common air heated "product vaporizers" are passive, with power only needed for instrumentation and controls (but this has inadequate output pressure to fill oxygen cylinders). "High pressure vaporizers" have an additional cryopump (placed between the bulk tank and the vaporizer) that enables filling of oxygen cylinders, but also requires additional power and is not commonly used at health facilities.

Storage and transport of liquid oxygen requires **less space than gaseous oxygen** (1 liter liquid oxygen (O_2) = 798 liters gaseous O_2[69]) and can, therefore, be cheaper, but it does require specialized tanker trucks and strict safety. Storage and handling of liquid oxygen is **strictly regulated** as the potential consequences from rupture, leak, or malfunction can be catastrophic. There are multiple regulatory standards for VIE design, fabrication, inspection, and testing (footnote 13).

VIEs are usually **owned by the gas company**, with facilities paying a leasing and/or service fee relative to the volume and frequency of refill. Installation costs, including all required infrastructure, may cost $10,000 to $100,000. Lease and/or service fees paid by facilities can be up to 40% of the installation cost annually, typically paid in monthly or quarterly installments (footnote 13).

---

67   1 liter liquid O_2 = 861 liters gaseous O_2.
68   Electrically heated vaporizers can also be used to prevent excessive icing in cold climates.
69   1 liter liquid oxygen = 0.7983 Nm³ at normal temperature and pressure (NTP), 101 kPa 20°C. http://www.cts-my.com/conversion.html.

Liquid oxygen suppliers often charge a premium for "medical" versus "industrial" oxygen, however, the additional actual costs are minimal when providing oxygen at scale. Investigative reporting has revealed irregularities and variation in how pricing is applied to the health sector.[70]

Gas companies typically coordinate the ordering and installation of VIEs, and prefabricated units can be installed and operational within 3–6 months from order. Installation requires infrastructure preparation to provide a level, thickly concreted base, and secure fencing—usually subcontracted by the gas company to local civil contractors.

VIE **maintenance** is provided by gas companies as part of the gas supply contract and requires highly trained gas technicians or engineers to perform preventive and corrective maintenance. Preventive maintenance is required quarterly.

Oxygen Cylinders

Oxygen cylinders are the most ubiquitous method of oxygen distribution and supply to many hospitals, but have significant practical and economic limitations. Cylinders are best suited for backup oxygen supply, transport, or for small facilities with low oxygen demand, but are often the primary oxygen source for larger facilities as well. They do not require power for operation.

Oxygen cylinders are heavy metal cylinders that **store oxygen gas at high pressure**. Oxygen cylinders can be **filled** off-site at cryogenic or PSA or VSA plants and transported to facilities on trucks, or filled on-site from PSA or VSA plants (or some high-pressure VIEs). Oxygen cylinders are available in a **range of sizes**, from small portable cylinders containing 50–1,000 liters of gaseous oxygen to large cylinders containing 3,000–10,000 liters that are moved around using trolleys (Figure 7).

Cylinders can be used to provide oxygen to individual (or groups of) patients or connected via a distribution manifold to supply a ward or entire hospital. **Distribution manifolds** include pressure regulation, and the main consideration is correct fit and integrity of the copper distribution piping to prevent leakage, which is common.[71] If located in a **patient area**, cylinders must be secured to prevent falling over and causing crush injuries. They can be used to supply oxygen directly to patients or used via other delivery devices such as ventilator or CPAP machines.

---

70   T. Prien et al. 2014. Oxygen 93: A New Option for European Hospitals. *British Journal of Anaesthesia*. 113(5). pp. 886–867. doi: 10.1093/bja/aeu358 [published online first: 19 October 2014]; A. J. Enoch et al. 2020. Variability in the Use of Pulse Oximeters with Children in Kenyan Hospitals: A Mixed-Methods Analysis. *PLoS Medicine*. 16(12). e1002987. doi: 10.1371/journal.pmed.1002987 [published online first: 1 January 2020]; M. Davies, L. Rios, and C. Giles. 2021. Oxygen Firms Accused of Intimidating Mexican Hospitals During Pandemic. *The Guardian*; M. Davies, A. Onwuzoo, and S. Mednick. 2020. Fighting for Breath: How the Medical Oxygen Industry Is Failing African Hospitals. *The Guardian*. 10 August.

71   S. R. Howie et al. 2009. Meeting Oxygen Needs in Africa: An Options Analysis from the Gambia. *Bulletin of the World Health Organization*. 87(10). pp. 763–771.

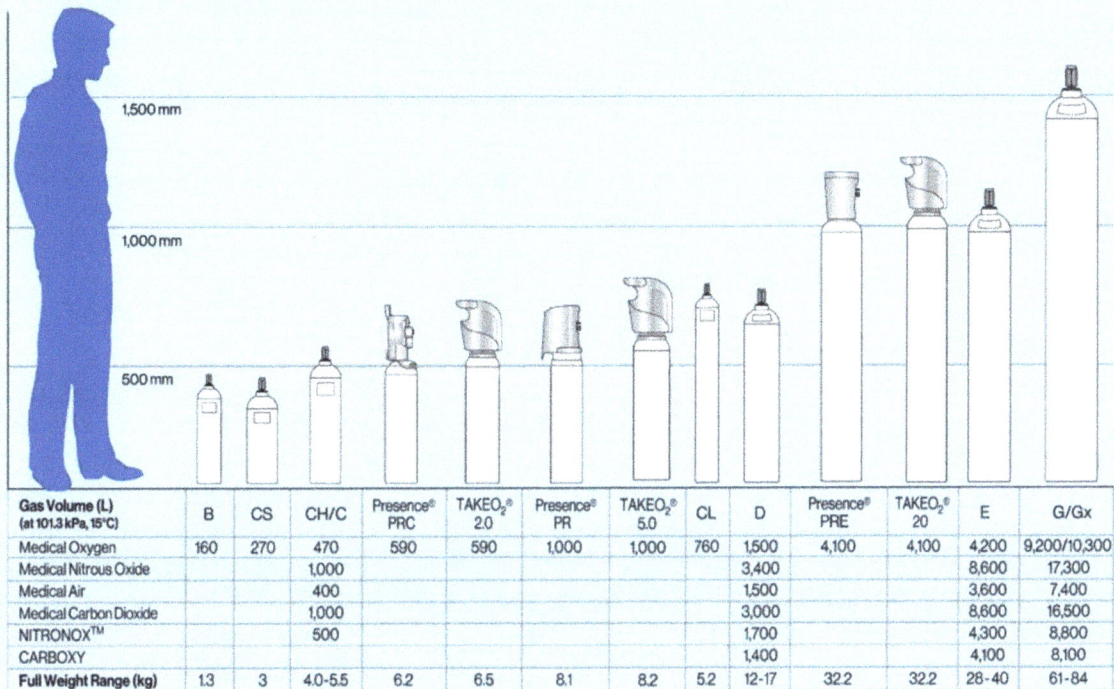

Figure 7: Example Oxygen Cylinder Size and Capacity

Gas Volume (L) (at 101.3 kPa, 15°C)	B	CS	CH/C	Presence® PRC	TAKEO₂® 2.0	Presence® PR	TAKEO₂® 5.0	CL	D	Presence® PRE	TAKEO₂® 20	E	G/Gx
Medical Oxygen	160	270	470	590	590	1,000	1,000	760	1,500	4,100	4,100	4,200	9,200/10,300
Medical Nitrous Oxide			1,000						3,400			8,600	17,300
Medical Air			400						1,500			3,600	7,400
Medical Carbon Dioxide			1,000						3,000			8,600	16,500
NITRONOX™			500						1,700			4,300	8,800
CARBOXY									1,400			4,100	8,100
Full Weight Range (kg)	1.3	3	4.0-5.5	6.2	6.5	8.1	8.2	5.2	12-17	32.2	32.2	28-40	61-84

kg = kilogram, L = liter, mm = millimeter.
Source: Air Liquide. http://agedcare.airliquidehealthcare.com.au/products/medical-oxygen/.

Cylinders must be used with a **pressure regulator** to enable supply of oxygen at a safe and appropriate pressure. The regulator apparatus includes valves and flowmeters, and these are susceptible to damage and leakage and must be handled with care. Different valves are used for different cylinders, including bullnose, pin-index, and integral.

Cylinders that contain oxygen are very similar to cylinders containing other compressed gases and should be **color-coded and clearly labeled** to prevent mix-up. ISO standards suggest black body with white shoulders, and newer standards are moving toward white bodies for all medical gases,[72] but coding varies by geography (and sometimes by supplier).

Oxygen cylinders should be manufactured, handled, and maintained with careful attention to safety as the **risks of puncture or fire** can be catastrophic. For example, a filled cylinder that falls over and cracks the valve head will be propelled through the air like a rocket, severely injuring and damaging anything in its way.

Oxygen cylinders can be **transported to facilities** on standard trucks, with appropriate signage and safety precautions. Supply is usually quick (hours to days), but can be longer during periods of high demand, and may be impossible to

---

[72] British Compressed Gases Association (BCGA). 2019. Technical Information Sheet 20 Medical Gases. *BCGA Policy on Colour Coding.* Derby, UK: BCGA.

transport to remote locations or during severe weather events (e.g., flooding over roads). Transport costs are a major component of oxygen cylinder costs and may be bundled into the supplier contract or borne by facilities.

Cylinders may be purchased by facilities or remain the property of the supplier through a lease agreement. **Costs for oxygen cylinders** are highly variable and sensitive to supply–demand and distance from filling station. Indicative costs for large "J" cylinder (6,800 liters): purchase $54 to $229; monthly rental $25 + deposit; refill $23 to $112 (footnote 13).

Oxygen cylinders require **minimal maintenance,** but should be visually inspected for damage every time they are refilled and used, and should undergo hydrostatic pressure testing every 5 years (expected life span: 20–25 years). Anecdotally, suppliers often fill old cylinders to less than maximal pressures due to concerns over their strength and in the absence of pressure testing.

Distribution Manifold and Reticulated Piped Distribution

Most established hospitals will aspire to a central reticulated gas pipe system, connected either to a bank of large oxygen cylinders, an on-site PSA or VSA plant, or a liquid oxygen storage tank (VIE). Piped systems can range from a simple distribution manifold connecting a few oxygen cylinders to outlets in a single ward, to far more elaborate piping connecting liquid oxygen storage to an entire hospital (with or without other medical gases).

The benefits of piped oxygen supply for health-care workers include easy access to continuous oxygen supply at each bedside without obstructive equipment in the clinical area or the need to call technicians to replace empty cylinders or find regulator attachments. The benefits of piped oxygen supply for technicians is a central location to manage and maintain oxygen supply without needing to drag equipment into clinical areas or between wards, and avoidance of additional equipment maintenance and power needs of concentrators.

Distribution manifolds include pressure regulation, and the main considerations are correct fit and integrity of the distribution piping network to prevent leakage. Poorly installed or maintained systems can leak to such an extent that the entire system is decommissioned, or that most oxygen is lost.

Distribution piping is typically done using medical-grade copper piping and welded connections, and indicative costs range from $1,500 to $2,000 per outlet in European and North American markets. Providers in other parts of the world can achieve more affordable prices as low as $300 to $400 using alternate piping or joining option (Case Study 6). However, regulatory requirements and standards vary between jurisdictions and may limit the applicability of some lower cost distribution piping initiatives.

Simple plastic tubing can be used for distribution of oxygen to patients at small scale—typically from a single oxygen concentrator to 2 to 5 patients via a flowmeter assembly enabling individually titrated oxygen to each patient. This may be most applicable to small facilities that primarily use low-flow oxygen from oxygen concentrators or cylinders and is particularly useful for newborns and small children who typically have low oxygen volume requirements.

Simple plastic tubing. Distributing oxygen from one cylinder to five pediatric beds (photo by Trevor Duke, Papua New Guinea).

CASE STUDY 6

Global – Innovation in Piped Distribution Systems

Piped oxygen distributions are a core part of hospital infrastructure, but can be a source of leaks, wastage, and inefficiency if they are not installed correctly and maintained. **Build Health International** (BHI) is a nonprofit organization that designs and builds health infrastructure—from small clinics to large hospitals—and they have installed oxygen systems in countries all over the world.

BHI uses local technician capacity and simplified technology to make piped oxygen more affordable, typically achieving 75% cost reduction compared with the United States market. For example, BHI technicians wash, clean, dry, and protect the copper piping themselves (rather than pay the premium for medical copper piping which comes precleaned and vacuum sealed) and use "ProPress" crimping to join pipes (rather than traditional welding).

Other strategies to improve affordability include design considerations, such as fewer terminal units per bed and not duplexing the entire system. However, this must be done with care to ensure that sections of the distribution system can be isolated in case of a ward-level leak, so that technicians can shut down and fix without compromising the entire system. Other engineering groups use cheaper alternatives to copper, such as PEX (cross-linked polyethylene) pipes. However, this may come with risk of damage or decay.

This case study shows that local capacity and innovation can make oxygen supply and distribution substantially more affordable and enable stronger patient outcomes. However, regulatory challenges and lack of globally accepted standards currently limit more widespread adoption.

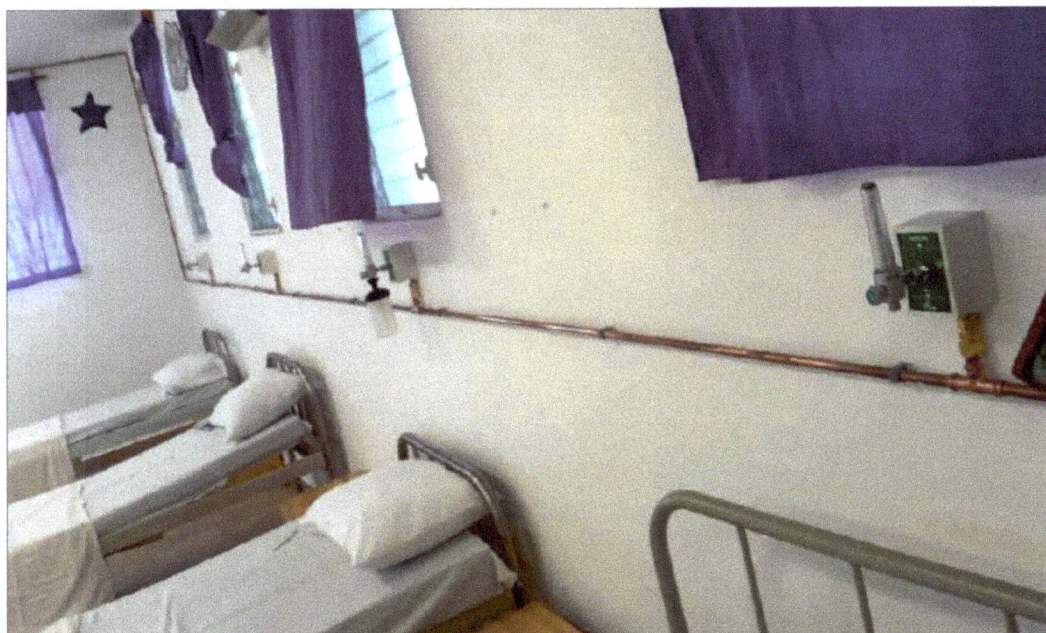

Piped distribution system. Making oxygen supply and distribution more affordable (photo by Build Health International).

6 Measurement, Forecasting, and Planning

Key Messages

✅ **Oxygen access** is ideally defined at the level of patients—the proportion of patients needing oxygen who receive it appropriately. Measuring oxygen access in terms of equipment availability alone will underestimate the supply gap and ignore the use gap.

✅ **Indicators** to track oxygen access should assess (i) oxygen supply at point-of-care, (ii) oximetry coverage, and (iii) cost. Higher-level systems indicators should also cover oxygen production capacity and procurement.

✅ **Forecasting oxygen needs** must consider factors relating to facility characteristics, patient use, distribution mechanisms, and natural variability. Data sources such as health management information system (HMIS) or district health information software (DHIS2), health facility master list, and medical equipment inventory can be leveraged to build oxygen need quantification at facility, regional, or national levels.

✅ **Decisions about oxygen supply and distribution** require both centralized coordination and localized contextual knowledge. Planning oxygen systems is a cyclical process of understanding the current situation, improving systems, and monitoring results to inform future action.

✅ **Planning efforts** must go beyond procurement and installation to include maintenance and repair, distribution, and workforce capacity building. Whole-of-life costing and effective planning and negotiation with suppliers at scale are essential.

Measuring Oxygen Access

Health systems approaches to **access to medicines** involves medication *availability*, *affordability*, *quality*, and *rational use.*[73] For oxygen access, this means quality oxygen therapy is available and affordable to those who need it, when they need it, and used in a safe and rational way.

Unlike other health areas (such as HIV, malaria, maternal health), there are no **routine or standardized oxygen indicators** or measurements of oxygen access resulting in severe lack of data to answer

(i)   How many patients require oxygen treatment, and how many patients actually receive it?

(ii)   How much oxygen is produced, distributed, and used by the medical sector?

(iii)   What is the oxygen access gap between need and supply?

(iv)   How much do oxygen services cost the health system and patients?

The lack of data on supply and demand is hindering local and global efforts to identify key bottlenecks and develop effective solutions. Existing service availability and provision assessments (e.g., Demographic Health Survey Service Provision Assessment; Service Availability and Readiness Assessment) have used a binary metric of oxygen availability measuring the presence of oxygen supply equipment (oxygen concentrators or cylinders) in facilities. However, asking only about oxygen equipment presence will massively underestimate the supply gap and will give no insight into whether oxygen is actually reaching the patients who need it (Figure 10, Table 3).[74]

Better metrics for assessing oxygen access, and quantifying the access gap, are being discussed by academics, the United Nations, and funding agencies. Our proposal is that these should holistically assess access by examining the entire oxygen service delivery chain—including oxygen production and procurement, oxygen supply at the points of care, how oxygen is used (particularly pulse oximetry coverage), and costs to patients and the health system (Figure 8, Table 2).[75] Integration of better oxygen access indicators in health facility surveys and health information systems assists facility staff, administrators, policy makers, and funders understand the "supply" and "use" gap and guide investment decisions (Case Study 7).

73   M. Bigdeli et al. 2013. Access to Medicines from a Health System Perspective. *Health Policy and Planning.* 28(7). pp. 692–704. doi: 10.1093/heapol/czs108 [published online first: 24 November 2012].

74   A. A. Bakare et al. 2020. Providing Oxygen to Children and Newborns: A Multi-Faceted Technical and Clinical Assessment of Oxygen Access and Oxygen Use in Secondary-Level Hospitals in Southwest Nigeria. *International Health.* doi: 10.1093/inthealth/ihz009; H. R. Graham et al. 2021. Measuring Oxygen Access: Lessons from Health Facility Assessments in Nigeria. *medRxiv.*

75   H. R. Graham et al. 2021. Measuring Oxygen Access: Lessons from Health Facility Assessments in Nigeria. *medRxiv.*

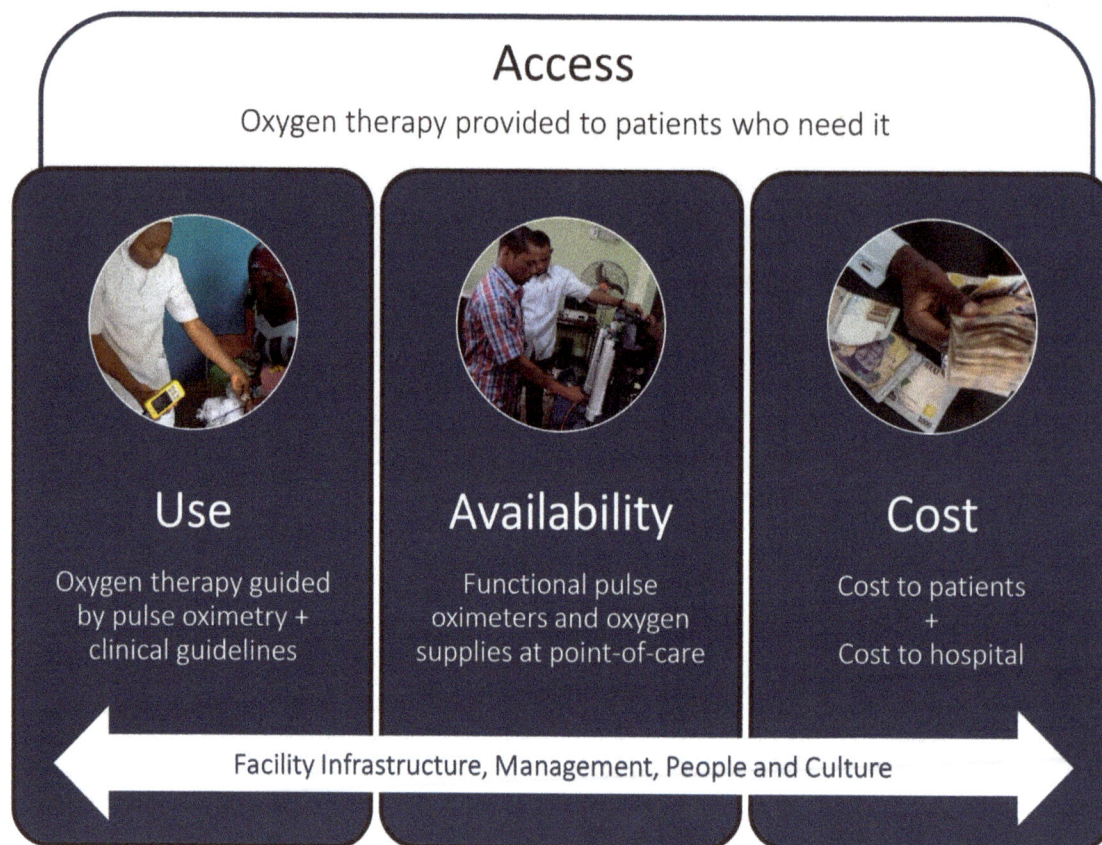

Figure 8: Key Indicators for Measuring Oxygen Access

Access
Oxygen therapy provided to patients who need it

Use
Oxygen therapy guided by pulse oximetry + clinical guidelines

Availability
Functional pulse oximeters and oxygen supplies at point-of-care

Cost
Cost to patients + Cost to hospital

Facility Infrastructure, Management, People and Culture

Source: H. R. Graham et al. 2021. Measuring Oxygen Access: Lessons from Health Facility Assessments in Nigeria. *medRxiv*.

Table 3: Summary of Most Useful Indicators of Oxygen Access

Domain	Indicator	Potential Sources

Use	• Proportion of patients with hypoxemia receiving oxygen therapy
	• Proportion of acutely unwell patients screened using pulse oximetry
	Additional considerations:
	  - presence of oxygen clinical guideline, including routine pulse oximetry
	  - rational use (oxygen provision with versus without indication)
	  - flow rates and duration of therapy (useful for quantification of oxygen need and quality improvement)
	  - equity between populations (hospital department, age, sex, ethnic background, socioeconomic status)
	  - training and skills of health-care workers
		Clinical audit, routine health information system, HCW survey

Continued on next page

Table 3 continued

Availability	• Proportion of wards with functional oxygen source and delivery devices
	• Proportion of wards with functional pulse oximeter and probes
	Additional considerations:
	  – pulse oximeter and oxygen source presence and function (including oxygen purity testing for oxygen concentrators)
	  – delivery devices (cannula, mask, CPAP, f/owmeter assembly, etc.)
	  – maintenance personnel (local capacity and access to expert help)
	  – equipment inventory and preventive maintenance schedules
	  – spare parts: access and cost
		Physical inspection+device testing, technician survey

Cost	• Daily cost of oxygen therapy to patients
	• Annual expenditure on oxygen equipment and maintenance/repairs
	Additional considerations:
	  – equity and nonpayment action (hospital department, age, poor)
	  – whole of life cycle (capital and operating costs): oxygen source, refill cost, spare parts and maintenance, power, consumables
		Patient's accounts and general finance ledger, administrator survey

CPAP = continuous positive airway pressure, HCW = health-care worker.

Source: H. R. Graham et al. 2021. Measuring Oxygen Access: Lessons from Health Facility Assessments in Nigeria. *medRxiv*.

CASE STUDY 7

Bangladesh – Integration of Oxygen Indicators in Health Information Systems

A national facility assessment in Bangladesh in 2020 revealed that 70% of hospitals lacked basic oxygen supplies in the maternal, pediatric, and newborn units. In response to this, the National Newborn Health Program and Integrated Management of Childhood Illness Program, supported by the United Nations Children's Fund (UNICEF) and the United States Agency for International Development, implemented a quality improvement program with a focus on pulse oximetry and oxygen therapy.

In addition to infrastructure improvements, capacity building, and strengthening of quality improvement processes, indicators for hypoxemia measurement and oxygen use were included in the national health management information system (DHIS2).

At the hospital level, indicators included the following:
  (i)   Number or proportion of children with oxygen saturation measured with a pulse oximeter
  (ii) Number or proportion of children with hypoxemia
  (iii) Number or proportion of children with hypoxia, severe pneumonia, or respiratory illness that received oxygen therapy
  (iv) Number of core clinical and technical staff trained on the use of oxygen therapy

At the primary care level, indicators included the following:
  (i)   Number or proportion of children with oxygen saturation measured with a pulse oximeter
  (ii) Number or proportion of children with hypoxemia

Continued on next page

Case Study 7 continued

These indicators were embedded alongside existing quality improvement processes and health information reporting systems, better representing child and newborn health within health monitoring and providing far more useful information on oxygen access.

This case study shows the importance of measuring what matters. Tracking these important oxygen access indicators enables hospital and health department staff to observe the effects of interventions and identify areas that needed additional attention.

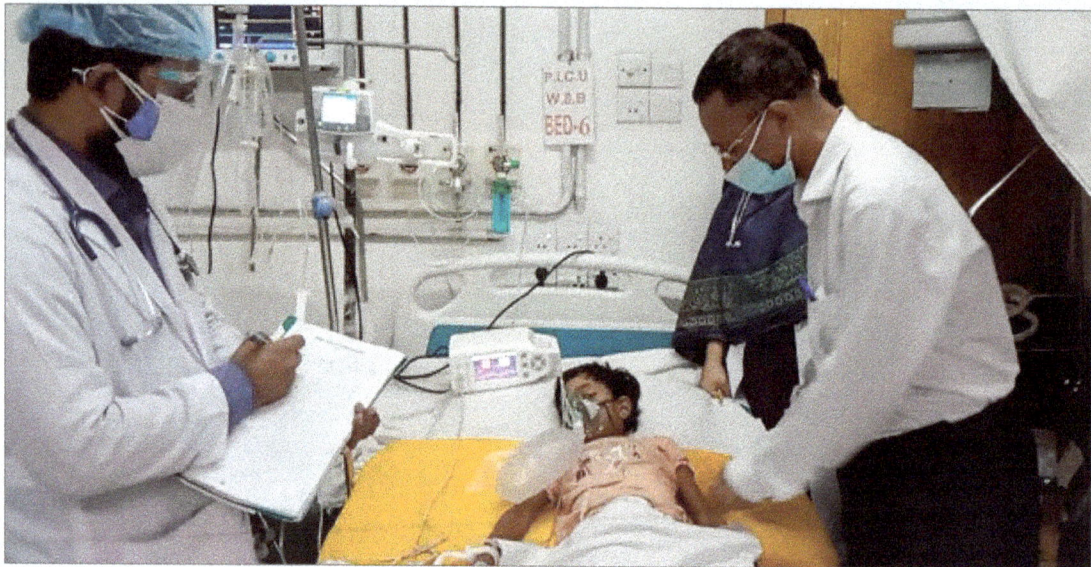

Oxygen in Bangladesh. Child receiving oxygen therapy (photo by UNICEF/L'IV Com Sàrl/Steiner).

Forecasting Oxygen Need

Oxygen need is calculated by volume (liters) based on average patient numbers (often constrained by the number of beds available), typical flow rates, and treatment duration for each type of patients. Four factors complicate forecasting oxygen need based on mean volume: (i) variability in the number of cases (e.g., COVID-19 case surge), (ii) poor health information data (e.g., number of admissions, hypoxemia prevalence), (iii) patient characteristics, and (iv) distribution between and within facilities.

Oxygen supply and distribution systems must be able to provide oxygen to patients at peak need. There is great variability in the volume of oxygen required at a facility, and the places and people it is used for. Oxygen requirements in a single facility vary substantially from day to night (e.g., elective surgery happens during the day), over days and weeks (e.g., random variation in admissions), seasonally (e.g., pneumonia season), and through epidemic surges (e.g., COVID-19). Modeling estimates show that in a busy district hospital, hourly oxygen need for child pneumonia is commonly more than three times what would be expected based on need averaged over months.[76] Variation is even greater in smaller facilities.

Oxygen supply systems based on local production (i.e., concentrators, PSA or VSA plants) must be sized for peak needs, as they lack the ability to store excess oxygen for later use. Oxygen supply systems that are based on local storage (i.e., liquid oxygen VIE, oxygen cylinders) do not need to be sized for peak needs,[77] as they can release additional volume for some period of time—but they will need to be more frequently filled during surges in need.

Oxygen supply and delivery systems must suit the case mix and population of each facility. The volume of oxygen used in adult intensive-care environments is substantially higher per patient than lower acuity wards or child or newborn ward settings. Similarly, the methods of delivery and required delivery apparatuses are also different. For example, neonatal units typically have many patients who require oxygen and use a variety of respiratory care devices (e.g., nasal cannulae, CPAP), but the volume of oxygen required per patient is much lower than in an adult high-dependency ward.

Larger facilities are typically able to **aggregate and manage variability in need** better than small facilities (footnote 76), particularly if they have a centralized oxygen distribution system that does not rely on moving equipment between wards. However, facilities that move cylinders or concentrators around to meet needs will need an oxygen supply capacity that is much higher than their overall mean requirements. All facilities will still face fluctuation in need—for example, during different seasons or disease outbreaks (e.g., influenza, COVID-19)—but their ability to predict consumption over time may vary substantially.

At a health systems level, COVID-19 has shown how variations in need and supply can impact entire provinces and countries—with major hospitals and entire hospital networks unable to access medical oxygen when it was needed. It has also highlighted challenges in how oxygen supply and distribution decisions are made, with centralized decision-making bodies able to trigger large-scale changes to increase oxygen supply, but still requiring localized understanding of context to get oxygen to facilities and patients effectively and equitably.

A number of **oxygen forecasting and planning tools** are now available for planners at the level of individual facilities, multiple facilities, and entire districts and country (Case Study 8). These are best used to help planners work with other stakeholders (e.g., clinicians, engineers, funders, suppliers) to map out needs and options. Many of the inputs will vary greatly between provinces and countries, including the types of oxygen services provided, the patient population served, and the costs of power, equipment, and personnel. The recommendations from the tool must also be considered in context, including existing oxygen system capacity and structure, access to local technical expertise, and ability to provide ongoing finance to maintain services.

---

76   B. D. Bradley et al. 2014. Estimating Oxygen Needs for Childhood Pneumonia in Developing Country Health Systems: A New Model for Expecting the Unexpected. *PLoS ONE.* 9(2). e89872. doi: http://dx.doi.org/10.1371/journal.pone.0089872.
77   Oversizing VIE plants will result in pressure buildup, off-gassing, and oxygen wastage.

CASE STUDY 8

Global – Tools for Forecasting Needs and Planning

The **UNICEF Oxygen System Planning tool** is an Excel-based tool for large-scale oxygen systems planning. Designed to be used at the national or provincial level, users can input specific data about individual health facilities or create generic model facilities. The tool requires many inputs and provides suggested "global" values for users who do not have local data. Inputs include hypoxemia prevalence and expected oxygen requirements at the level of wards (e.g., pediatric, adult, intensive care unit), admission numbers, existing infrastructure (e.g., power, oxygen piping), and cost data for energy, equipment (cylinder, concentrator, pressure swing adsorption (PSA) or vacuum swing adsorption (VSA) plant, oximeter), accessories, consumables, and overheads; it can be run over varying planning periods (years). The model also allows users to input data about existing PSA or VSA plants (including location), but does not currently include liquid oxygen options (a soon-to-be released version of the tool will include liquid oxygen). The model produces recommendations about most appropriate mix of supply technologies, and estimated capital expenditure (CAPEX) and operational expenditure (OPEX) costs.

UNICEF Oxygen System Planning tool: https://www.unicef.org/innovation/documents/oxygen-system-planning-tool.

The **PATH Quantification and Costing tools** are Excel-based tools for planning **oxygen supply** and **pulse oximetry** (separate tools) in one or multiple hospitals. The tools include prepopulated data for a small number of countries and prepopulated assumptions about oxygen requirements per bed, costs, and others that operate in the background. The tools calculate oxygen demand (volume) and number of recommended oximeters based on data from users about the mean number and type of beds (general, added services, critical care) at different facility levels. Users can then view different supply options (concentrator, cylinder, PSA or VSA plant, liquid) and explore the CAPEX and OPEX costs for a different technology mix.

PATH Qualification and Costing tools: https://www.path.org/resources/quantification-and-costing-tools/.

The **Open Critical Care Oxygen Supply and Demand calculator** is a simple online tool designed to be used at facility or ward level. By inputting patient load numbers and types of respiratory support provided, the calculator will estimate daily oxygen volume required. The supply calculator allows users to add details of the oxygen source, including particular makes and models of PSA or VSA plants, concentrators, cylinders, and liquid gas vacuum-insulated evaporators.

Open Critical Care Oxygen Supply and Demand calculator: https://opencriticalcare.org/oxygen-supply-demand-calculator/.

Planning

Planning oxygen systems improvements will vary by context and depending on the level of planning (e.g., individual or small groups of hospitals versus district or national level). At a macro level, oxygen systems strengthening requires consideration of all the major health systems building blocks: service delivery, health workforce, health information systems, access to essential medicines and devices, financing, and leadership and governance.[78] At a micro level, these same factors are often discussed as part of quality improvement: plan, do, study, and act.

---

[78]   WHO. 2010. *Monitoring the Building Blocks of Health Systems: A Handbook of Indicators and Their Measurement Strategies.* Geneva.

A comprehensive approach to oxygen systems strengthening typically involves gathering information, identifying priorities for action, implementing, monitoring, and adjusting. And it considers action across the program cycle—quantification, procurement, distribution, maintenance, clinical practice, capacity building—including at policy and practice levels. Too often, major investments are made to address single deficits (e.g., oxygen production capacity) without understanding how it fits within the broader oxygen ecosystem (and health system).

In addition to the previously mentioned assessment, quantification tools, and proposed oxygen access indicators, there are an increasing number of resources with **procurement**. The major opportunity here is for health managers to accurately aggregate demand to negotiate better access and contract conditions and some governments have centralized procurement systems in which oxygen devices can be integrated (Case Study 10).

Cost is a critical component of planning oxygen systems improvements and different options for oxygen supply present vastly different CAPEX and OPEX profiles. Whole-of-life costs can be very opaque and vary greatly between geographies due to market access and conditions, regulatory requirements, logistical supply challenges, and many other reasons. Planning tools (Case Study 9) can assist decision-makers with a framework to consider the cost implications of various choices, but rely heavily on local cost data and results depend heavily on decision-makers' ability to plan and negotiate with suppliers at scale.

Some of the major planning gaps for oxygen systems are in the management of oxygen infrastructure following procurement and the distribution and use of oxygen for patients. **Maintenance and repair** systems for biomedical and larger equipment are weak in many countries and are often overloaded and inadequately supported to deal with influxes of new equipment. **Distribution mechanisms** to get oxygen from the site of production to the bedside are similarly neglected from planning strategies, particularly for smaller and more remote facilities. **Technical and health-care workforce capacity building** is often mentioned in planning, but inadequately funded or integrated into ongoing training programs, and this is a particular problem in places that already have severe deficiencies in skilled workers. In the context of COVID-19 investments, many partners worry that new oxygen concentrators and plants will fail to deliver their promised benefits without substantial and sustained support for the maintenance, repair, distribution, and workforce elements of these oxygen systems.

CASE STUDY 9

Global – Planning Steps and Tools, PATH Example

The PATH Oxygen Planning Toolkit aims to help decision-makers step through essential questions in the planning and implementation cycle.[79]
   (i)   Understanding the oxygen environment
     • *What are the oxygen needs at the facility level?* Hypoxemia prevalence. Treatment guidelines and services. Variation across levels of facility and geographically.
     • *What is the use environment for oxygen?* Current oxygen supply and use practices, procedures, and infrastructure. Workforce capacity.

Continued on next page

---

79   PATH. 2020. *Optimizing Oxygen Access and Reliability: Opportunities for Scaling Access and Applications to Other Medical Devices.* Seattle.

Case Study 9 continued

(ii)   Mapping the policy framework
   - *Has oxygen delivery been included in appropriate national and subnational policies and guidelines?* Clinical guidelines. Essential medicines and equipment. Regulatory requirements and safety standards.
   - *How are the oxygen delivery systems currently financed?* Capital expenditure and operational expenditure. Cost-recovery mechanisms. Levels and domains of financial responsibility. Costs to patients, facilities, and health system.

(iii) Clarifying the supply situation
   - *What is the current supply management landscape for oxygen technologies and supplies?* Current availability and supply chain mapping of oxygen equipment, including accessories and spare parts. Additional supply options.
   - *Do standard technical specifications exist to guide the selection of quality-assured, appropriate, and affordable products?* Comparison of existing technology to local and global standards.

(iv) Scaling-up oxygen delivery systems
   - *What mechanisms are in place for strengthening stakeholder coordination and supporting implementation?* Policy makers, implementing partners, professional associations, technical experts, funders.
   - *How is the ongoing availability and functionality of oxygen delivery monitored across communities and facilities?* Integrating oxygen indicators into routine health and biomedical information systems.

Figure 9: Oxygen Delivery Toolkit Resources Life Cycle

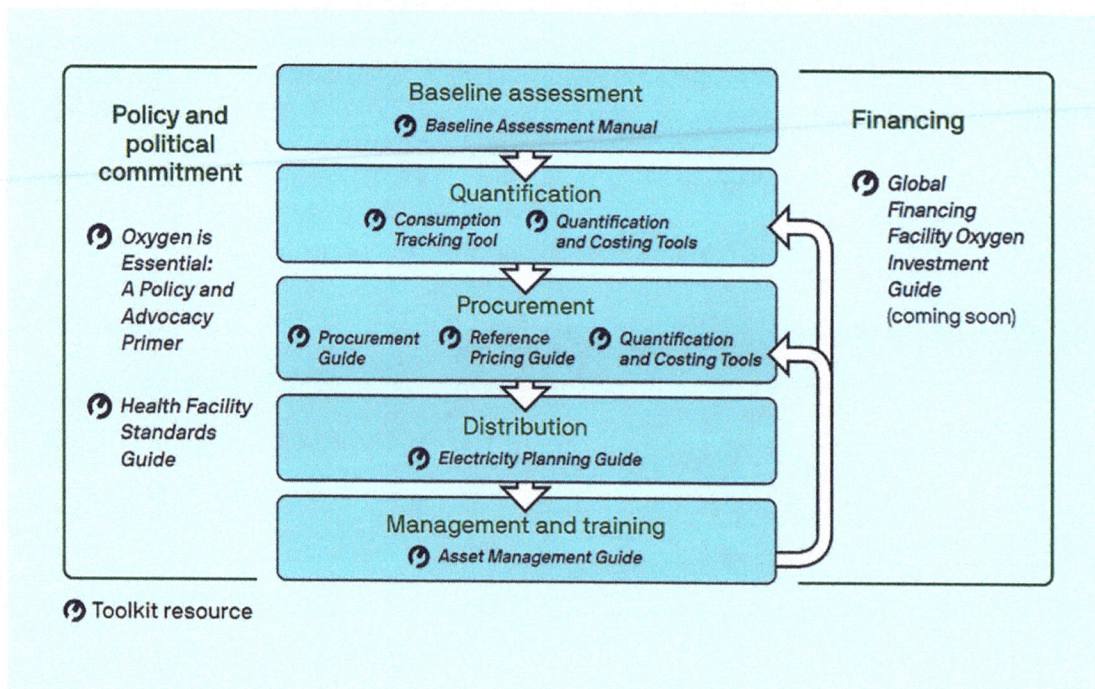

Source: PATH. 2020. *Optimizing Oxygen Access and Reliability: Opportunities for Scaling Access and Applications to Other Medical Devices.* Seattle.

CASE STUDY 10

Indonesia – Procurement and Asset Management

Indonesia has a strong supply system for medical equipment and national regulations and guidelines for oxygen delivery technology and medical gas systems, including specifications for what is appropriate at each level of the health system. The national Application Infrastructure and Medical Devices (Aplikasi Sarana Prasarana dan Alat Kesehatan [ASPAK]) enables efficient tracking of device deployment (Figure 10). The Ministry of Health (via the National Public Procurement Agency [Lembaga Kebijakan Pengadaan Barang or LKPP] administers an online procurement system (e-Katalog) to facilitate coordinated ordering of medical products at a negotiated price. Through this, the LKPP issues requests to device suppliers, who bid to have their devices included in the catalog, and then negotiate with suppliers to secure a competitive price for bulk purchase, and ensure devices meet quality standards. Facilities can then purchase devices through the e-Katalog with confidence.

This case study shows how a centralized equipment procurement and tracking system can serve a decentralized health service system. However, a review by PATH found that there were challenges in its execution, with many facilities procuring equipment outside the online platform and a missed potential for further price reductions for products listed on the e-Katalog.[80] In practice, logistics, transport, and cost challenges resulted in much poorer oxygen access in smaller facilities in more rural areas.

Figure 10: Percentage of Facilities in Indonesia by Province with Access to Oxygen, Heat Map

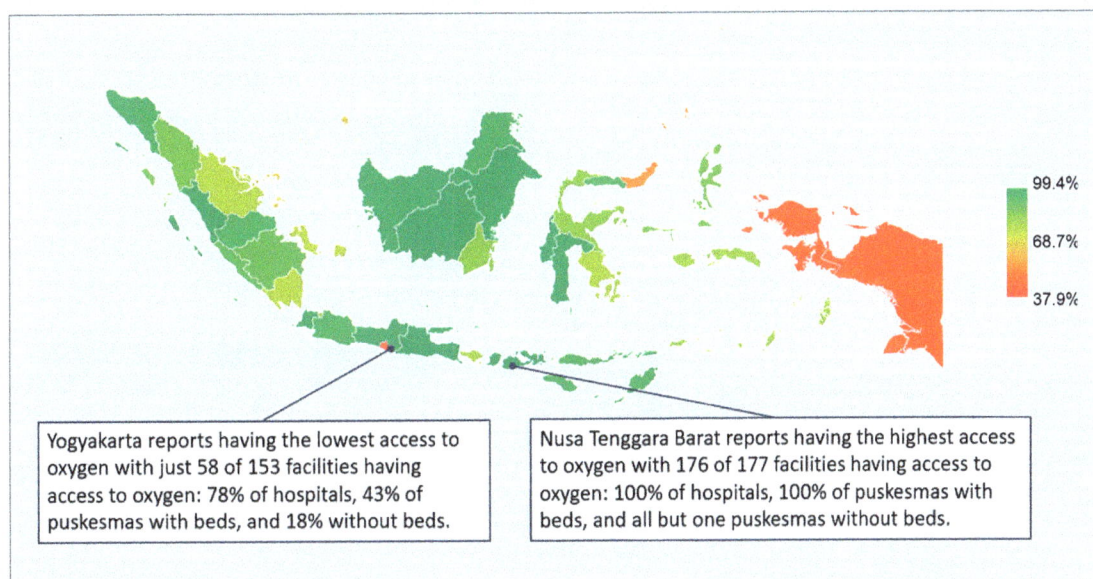

99.4%

68.7%

37.9%

Yogyakarta reports having the lowest access to oxygen with just 58 of 153 facilities having access to oxygen: 78% of hospitals, 43% of puskesmas with beds, and 18% without beds.

Nusa Tenggara Barat reports having the highest access to oxygen with 176 of 177 facilities having access to oxygen: 100% of hospitals, 100% of puskesmas with beds, and all but one puskesmas without beds.

Source: PATH. 2018. *Market Assessment and Recommendations to Increase Access to Oxygen and Pulse Oximetry in Indonesia.* Seattle: PATH. https://path.azureedge.net/media/documents/Indonesia_Country_Report.pdf.

7 Opportunities for Investment

Opportunities

Ensuring that patients who need oxygen are identified and treated appropriately depends on a complex system. This guidance note has highlighted current weaknesses and challenges in the systems that produce, distribute, and provide oxygen to patients. But this also presents enormous opportunities to support national effort to

(i)   Coordinate oxygen systems planning, procurement, distribution, and maintenance at a larger scale; and using better data and planning, and monitoring and evaluation tools.
(ii) Increase supply of bulk oxygen in areas that struggle from limited supply options or competition; and improve the distribution of oxygen to populations that have been historically neglected.
(iii) Strengthen maintenance, repair, and biomedical capacity for oxygen; and imagine better systems to keep equipment functioning longer.
(iv) Support health-care workers with the tools and skills to use pulse oximetry and oxygen better.
(v)   Use financial tools to de-risk and enable innovative oxygen supply, distribution and use models, and leverage off other investments (e.g., COVID-19).

Opportunities to strengthen oxygen systems can be mapped to the **values and principles mapped out in ADB's Strategy 2030 and the priorities in ADB's Operational Plan for Health.**[81] They require country-focused approaches that are focused on equality, especially for rural and remote access. They include great potential to integrate health solutions with other sectors—particularly power—and see health sector investments contribute to economic growth. They offer opportunity to support innovative technology and service models pioneered by local entrepreneurs.

---

[81] ADB. 2015. *Health in Asia and the Pacific: A Focused Approach to Address the Health Needs of ADB Developing Member Countries. Operational Plan for Health, 2015–2020*. Manila.

Financing and Implementation Support

The following opportunities are far from complete, but may give a sense of some of the actions ADB can take to support country oxygen scale-up strategies for the medium to long term.

Table 4: Opportunities for ADB Action to Support Country-Level Oxygen Systems Strengthening, Utilize Various Financing Mechanisms and Models, and Promote Knowledge Generation and Dissemination

	Potential Examples
Capacity development technical assistance	
National oxygen scale-up strategies	Support to create and funding to enact comprehensive national plans. Partnership with WHO, UNICEF, and other implementers supporting governments to strengthen oxygen systems.
Coordination and procurement	Support aggregation of demand across numerous facilities to secure better contracts with suppliers and distributors. Support development and application of centralized procurement platforms.
Increase liquid oxygen production and distribution for medical use	Coinvest or underwrite expansion of oxygen production for medical use. Coinvest or underwrite expansion of oxygen distribution for medical use.
Supply chain and distribution	Support development and deployment of supply chain tools, including tracking technology. Encourage innovative distribution approaches and comprehensive oxygen-as-a-service models.
Maintenance and repair systems	Fund the entire maintenance framework including people, tools and testing equipment, spare parts, and information management systems. Secure better service contracts for long-term maintenance.
Learning and innovation	Support evidence generation on what strategies improve oxygen supply and patient access in what contexts, and why. Foster innovation in technology and service provision systems.
Biomedical workforce capacity	Ensure there are paid biomedical engineering positions at key hospitals, upskilling biomedical capacity on oxygen, and integrating with other biomedical services.
Health-care workforce capacity	Build the health workforce, particularly nursing; upskill health-care workers on pulse oximetry and oxygen, integrating into standardized clinical charts and guidelines.
Remote facilities	Support establishment of risk-pooling insurance that enables more remote facilities to access oxygen services. Support rural energy-health programs that integrate improved power with oxygen services.
Infrastructure	Support associated infrastructure, including power and transport.

Coninued on next page

Table 4 continued

Financing mechanisms and models	
Loans and concessional financing	To government, district health offices, or private sector—to invest in the key actions contained in this table.
Subsidies	Concessional financing to extend oxygen supply and maintenance services to more remote areas and smaller facilities.
Leasing agreements	Financing small and medium-sized enterprises that produce, supply, and operate oxygen plants to enable them to expand their services and carry greater assets.
Collateral investments and/or guarantees	Stimulate new large-scale investments in oxygen production and establish distribution and maintenance services at scale. Enable larger volume, longer-term contracts between the health sector and gas companies.
Integrated financing	Finance renewable power microgrids in rural areas with oxygen plant as a core customer.
Leveraging or coinvestment	Build from COVID-19 emergency response investments to support integration into health systems and strengthening of information systems and essential services for maintenance, repair, and clinical care.
Knowledge generation and dissemination	
Regional cooperative activities	Convene regional working groups to tackle international challenges and opportunities with oxygen supply.
Direct research	Pilot projects to address systems-level oxygen systems challenges. Do implementation research to test strategies for extending services to rural areas, or innovative maintenance models.
Measurement and monitoring	Support the use (and adaptation and improvement) of planning and M&E tools at national and regional scales. Integrate oxygen indicators in health and logistics management information systems (HIS, LMIS).
Market analysis and shaping	Define the complexity, fragmentation, monopolization of oxygen supply and distribution markets.
Regulation and consumer protection	Act to prevent and break up monopolies on oxygen supply. Support smaller suppliers and/or distributors (e.g., "merchant suppliers") to enter markets and/or compete. Target pricing for health sector.

COVID-19 = coronavirus disease, HIS = health management information system, LMIS = logistics management information system, M&E = monitoring and evaluation, UNICEF = United Nations Children's Fund, WHO = World Health Organization.

ADB. 2015. *Health in Asia and the Pacific: A Focused Approach to Address the Health Needs of ADB Developing Member Countries. Operational Plan for Health, 2015–2020*. Manila.

Leveraging COVID-19 Investments

The COVID-19 pandemic has heightened global awareness of the importance of, and deficiencies in, medical oxygen systems. Investments have flowed in at small and large scales, directly and via coordinated global mechanism. Substantial investments in oxygen have been made through the COVID-19 Access to COVID-19 Tools Accelerator (Figure 11). Launched in April 2020, this supported a coordinated effort to fight COVID-19. Oxygen response was somewhat slow, but became faster when the COVID-19 Oxygen Emergency Taskforce was launched in February 2021, led by Unitaid and the Wellcome Trust.

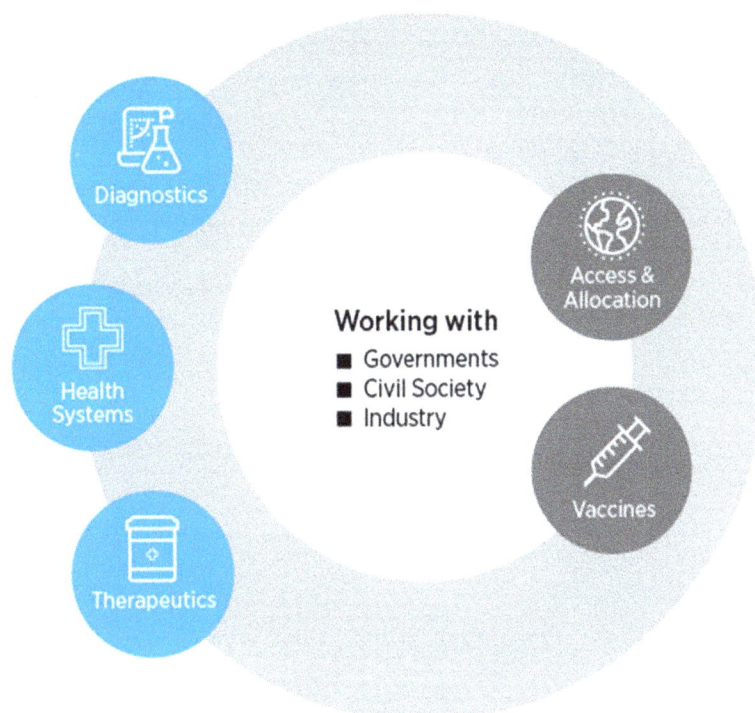

Figure 11: COVID-19 Access to COVID-19 Tools Accelerator

Working with
- Governments
- Civil Society
- Industry

Diagnostics

Health Systems

Therapeutics

Access & Allocation

Vaccines

Source: The Global Fund.

The Global Fund has been the largest oxygen funder to date, disbursing $472 million to 75 countries for oxygen as of 29 September 2021, and it updates regularly. But its funding has run out. Unitaid and Wellcome have contributed an additional $20 million. Funding for oxygen from other sources is less clear, possibly $10 million from UNICEF and WHO, and $50 million to $100 million from the World Bank (based on personal correspondence with Leith Greenslade on 29 September 2021).

However, this investment is far below what is needed and has largely been spent on the procurement and installation of oxygen plants and oxygen concentrators. Evidence clearly shows that without a concerted effort to strengthen the underlying systems to maintain, repair, and provide clinical services, the condition of newly purchased equipment will deteriorate and investments will fail to reach their potential impact. This presents a unique opportunity to support longer-term systems change that will leverage recent investments for greater impact.

Partnerships

There are many partners in United Nations agencies, and the nonprofit, academic, and private sectors that are actively working and collaborating around oxygen access. Many of these partners have been referenced or featured in case studies in this guidance note, and some have provided direct input for this guidance note's content. The following list is by no means comprehensive, but highlights some of the current activities of key partners that may be eager to work with ADB.

- The **World Health Organization** (WHO) has led the development and distribution of many normative guidance documents covering clinical and technical aspects relating to oxygen. WHO is closely involved at country and regional levels in Africa and the Asia and Pacific regions in providing technical support regarding oxygen.
- **UNICEF** has led the way in procurement and product specifications for many oxygen-related products. UNICEF is closely involved at country and regional levels in Africa and the Asia and Pacific regions in providing technical support regarding oxygen.
- **Clinton Health Access Initiative** (CHAI) and **PATH** have been supporting countries in Africa and the Asia and Pacific regions to develop and implement oxygen strategies and have produced many of the guidance materials referenced in this guidance note.
- **Unitaid** cohosts the Access to COVID-19 Tools Accelerator therapeutics pillar and the COVID-19 Oxygen Emergency Taskforce. Unitaid has funded and leveraged support for innovative approaches to oxygen services, including maintenance, and negotiated an agreement with major liquid oxygen suppliers (with CHAI).

8 Conclusions

> **"We don't just need more investment in public health. We must also rethink how we value health."**
>
> — Dr. Tedros Adhanom Ghebreyesus,
> WHO Director General, World Health Assembly,
> 13 November 2020

Health is central to the human experience and social and economic development.[82] If the coronavirus disease (COVID-19) pandemic taught us anything, it is that health, economics, and society are integrally related. Global calls to invest in pandemic preparedness have become increasingly loud and urgent.[83]

Within this context, COVID-19 has shone a spotlight on the human cost of weak oxygen systems and destroyed any remaining excuses for inaction. Strengthening oxygen systems is a cost-effective investment that saves lives. Strengthening oxygen systems has a broad range of beneficiaries with diverse health conditions—from premature newborns to older adults with pneumonia, from children with severe infections to young adults requiring surgery, from trauma victims to COVID-19 patients. Strengthening oxygen systems complements efforts to improve quality of care at every level of the health system and across infectious disease and noncommunicable disease silos.

The good news is that, collectively, we know most of what is needed to improve oxygen systems. We know that improved coordination and distribution of existing supplies can improve access to many smaller facilities. We know that measuring simple indicators will enable decision-makers to make better decisions, use money more efficiently, and get oxygen to those who need it. We know that basic investment in the people and systems

---

82 WHO Council on the Economics of Health for All. 2021. *The WHO Council on the Economics of Health for All: Manifesto.*
83 G20 High Level Independent Panel. 2021. *A Global Deal for our Pandemic Age: Report of the G20 High Level Independent Panel on Financing the Global Commons for Pandemic Preparedness and Response.*

responsible for maintaining and repairing oxygen equipment will increase their productivity and extend life spans. We know that simple tools like pulse oximetry and training and support for frontline health-care workers can be the difference between saving a life and losing one.

With more supporters for oxygen systems strengthening today than ever in history, we can make oxygen access to the last mile a reality. These tasks are simple, but not easy. They require cooperation between governments, funders, implementers, and those providing technical support. This guidance note provides some ideas and resources to progress work in the Asia and Pacific region, including specific opportunities for ADB support. And it contains hope that the grim lessons from the current crisis will catalyze the collective political will and ambition needed to achieve oxygen access for all.

9 Resources

- A2O2 Resource Library. This Access to Oxygen (A2O2) Resource Library has been developed as a central place to host a comprehensive set of both global and country-specific tools, guidance, data, publications, policies, protocols, and advocacy resources for oxygen scale-up. Compiled by PATH, Clinton Health Access Initiative (CHAI), Every Breath Counts coalition (EBC) via the Gates-funded COVID-19 Respiratory Care Response Coordination Project. https://a2o2resources.org/.
  - A2O2: Accelerating Access to Oxygen Meeting Summary. https://path.azureedge.net/media/documents/A2O2_Meeting_Report.pdf.
- UNICEF Oxygen Supply Program. https://www.unicef.org/innovation/oxygen-therapy.
  - UNICEF Oxygen Resources Library. https://bit.ly/OxygenResources.
- WHO Oxygen Access Scale-Up. https://www.who.int/initiatives/oxygen-access-scale-up.
  - WHO. 2021. Technical Consultation on Oxygen Scale Up for COVID-19.
  - PAHO. 2022. Good Practices in the Rational and Effective Use of Oxygen.
- CHAI Oxygen Program. https://www.clintonhealthaccess.org/our-programs/oxygen/.
- PATH Oxygen Program. https://www.path.org/programs/market-dynamics/increasing-access-safe-oxygen/.
  - COVID-19 and Oxygen: Resource Library. https://www.path.org/programs/market-dynamics/covid-19-and-oxygen-resource-library/Advocacy.
- Every Breath Counts Resources Library. https://stoppneumonia.org/advocate-resources/library/.
- PATH. 2020. Oxygen Is Essential: A Policy and Advocacy Primer. https://www.path.org/resources/oxygen-is-essential-a-policy-and-advocacy-primer/.
- PATH. 2020. Markets Matter: Closing the Oxygen Gap Campaign: Campaign Messages and Resources around Closing the Oxygen Gap in Countries. https://spark.adobe.com/page/BsriDuUA3ZaQU/.
- PATH. 2019. Oxygen as a Utility Report: An Innovative Model for Increasing Access to Oxygen in Low- and Middle-Income Countries. https://www.path.org/resources/oxygen-utility-report/.
- Every Breath Counts Coalition (EBC) Oxygen Partners List. https://docs.google.com/spreadsheets/d/19KC17OZ_teDIeB_AQOZRQ4UFsulwoT3X9K4O_wn3gKA/edit#gid=0.
- Duke, T. et al. 2010. Oxygen Is an Essential Medicine: A Call for International Action. IJTLD. https://pubmed.ncbi.nlm.nih.gov/20937173/.

Planning and Forecasting

General Planning

- PATH. 2020. *Oxygen Delivery Toolkit: Resources to Plan and Scale Medical Oxygen.* https://www.path.org/programs/market-dynamics/oxygen-delivery-toolkit/.
  - Oxygen Is Essential: A Policy and Advocacy Primer. https://www.path.org/resources/oxygen-is-essential-a-policy-and-advocacy-primer/.
  - Health Facility Standards Guide.
  - Baseline Assessment Manual.
  - Consumption Tracking Tool.
  - Procurement Guide.
  - Reference Pricing Guide.
  - Electricity Planning Guide.
  - Asset Management Guide.
  - Global Financing Facility Medical Oxygen Investment Guide.
- Smith, L. et al. 2020. *COVID-19 and Oxygen: Selecting Supply Options in LMICs that Balance Immediate Needs with Long-Term Cost-Effectiveness. CGD Note.* https://www.cgdev.org/publication/covid-19-and-oxygen-selecting-supply-options-lmics-balance-immediate-needs-long-term.

Measurement

- Graham, H. R. et al. 2021. Measuring Oxygen Access: Lessons from Health Facility Assessments in Lagos, Nigeria. *BMJ Global Health.* https://pubmed.ncbi.nlm.nih.gov/34344666/.
- Bradley, B. D. et al. 2014. Estimating Oxygen Needs for Childhood Pneumonia in Developing Country Health Systems: A New Model for Expecting the Unexpected. *PLoS ONE.* https://pubmed.ncbi.nlm.nih.gov/24587089/.

Quantification and Planning Tools

- UNICEF Oxygen System Planning Tool helps countries map out oxygen equipment needs at health facilities across the country. It is also useful for COVID-19 response planning. The algorithm and global level inputs were informed by the UNICEF advisory committee and technical review group of experts. https://www.unicef.org/innovation/documents/oxygen-system-planning-tool.
- PATH Oxygen Quantification and Costing Tool. https://www.path.org/resources/quantification-and-costing-tools/.
- USAID–UCSF–WFSA Open Critical Care Oxygen Supply and Demand Calculator. https://opencriticalcare.org/oxygen-supply-demand-calculator/.
- WHO COVID-19 Essential Supplies Forecasting Tool (ESFT) includes oxygen quantification, but is focused on COVID-19 demand. https://www.who.int/publications/i/item/WHO-2019-nCoV-Tools-Essential-forecasting-2021-1.
- WHO Needs Assessment for Medical Devices. 2011.
- WHO Health Technology Assessment of Medical Devices. 2011.
- WHO Essential Surgical Care (IMEESC) Toolkit: Tool for Situational Analysis to Assess Emergency and Essential Surgical Care. 2009.
- WHO Tools for COVID-19. https://www.who.int/emergencies/diseases/novel-coronavirus-2019/technical-guidance/covid-19-critical-items.
  - WHO Essential Supplies Forecasting Tool.
  - WHO Biomedical Equipment Inventory Tool.
- WHO. 2020. Biomedical Equipment for COVID-19 Case Management – Inventory Tool: Interim Guidance. https://www.who.int/publications/i/item/WHO-2019-nCov-biomedical-equipment-inventory-2020.1.

Procurement

- UNICEF Supply Catalogue. https://supply.unicef.org/.
- United National Office for Project Service UN Web Buy Plus. https://unwebbuyplus.org/.
- WHO Emergency Global Supply Chain System (COVID-19). https://www.who.int/publications/m/item/emergency-global-supply-chain-system-covid-19-catalogue.
- PATH Respiratory Care Equipment Market Report: A Preliminary Guide to Available Suppliers with Capacity to Provide Equipment for Respiratory Care. https://www.path.org/resources/respiratory-care-equipment-market-report/.

- PATH Respiratory Care Equipment Procurement Options: Summary Brief Highlighting Respiratory Care Equipment Procurement Options and Organizations That Play a Pivotal Role in Financing, Coordinating, and Conducting such Procurements. https://www.path.org/resources/respiratory-care-equipment-procurement-options/.

Equipment and Maintenance

General

- PATH/CHAI Oxygen Generation and Storage: Concise Primer for Decision-Makers Who Govern, Lead, Support, or Manage Health Systems and Their Associated Facilities. https://www.path.org/resources/oxygen-generation-and-storage/.
- PATH/CHAI Business Models in Respiratory Care: An Overview of Four Prevailing Business Models for Oxygen Production, Storage, Distribution, and Delivery. https://www.path.org/resources/business-models-respiratory-care/.
- Graham, H. R. et al. 2020. *Improving Hospital Oxygen Systems for COVID-19 in Low-Resource Settings: Lessons from the field.* GHSP. https://pubmed.ncbi.nlm.nih.gov/33361248/ https://pubmed.ncbi.nlm.nih.gov/33361248/.

Technical Specifications

- WHO. 2020. Technical Specifications for Pressure Swing Adsorption (PSA) Oxygen Plants. https://www.who.int/publications/i/item/WHO-2019-nCoV-PSA_Specifications-2020.1.
- WHO. 2020. Oxygen Sources and Distribution for COVID-19 Treatment Centres. https://www.who.int/publications/i/item/oxygen-sources-and-distribution-for-covid-19-treatment-centres.
- WHO. 2015. Technical Specifications and Guidance for Oxygen Concentrators. https://www.who.int/publications/i/item/9789241509886.
- WHO–UNICEF. 2019. Technical Specifications and Guidance for Oxygen Therapy Devices. https://apps.who.int/iris/handle/10665/329874.
- WHO. 2016. Technical Specifications of Neonatal Resuscitation Devices. https://apps.who.int/iris/handle/10665/206540.
- WHO. 2020. Priority Medical Devices List for the COVID-10 Response and Associated Technical Specifications. https://apps.who.int/iris/handle/10665/336745.
- WHO. 2020. Biomedical Equipment for COVID-19 Case Management – Inventory Tool: Interim Guidance. https://apps.who.int/iris/handle/10665/332777.
- WHO. 2020. Technical Specifications for Invasive and Non-Invasive Ventilators for COVID-19. https://apps.who.int/iris/handle/10665/331792.
- UCSF Open Oximetry Transparently Reports Function of Pulse Oximeters to Better Empower Users and Purchasers. https://openoximetry.org/oximeters/.

Capacity Assessment

- WHO. 2020. Biomedical Equipment for COVID-19 Case Management – Inventory Tool: Interim Guidance. https://www.who.int/publications/i/item/WHO-2019-nCov-biomedical-equipment-inventory-2020.1.
- Graham, H. R. et al. 2021. *Measuring Oxygen Access: Lessons from Health Facility Assessments in Lagos, Nigeria.* https://pubmed.ncbi.nlm.nih.gov/34344666/.

Maintenance

- Assist International Library of Resources for Oxygen Equipment Technicians. https://drive.google.com/drive/folders/1G1oXFbOpJRB1Ujo_mrnHejtNwAkA4WfY.
- Assist International Biomedical Technician Training Course for Concentrator Maintenance. https://www.stanesglobal.com/course?courseid=biomedical-equipment-technician-training.
- Oxygen Hub: Innovative Financing via Maintenance Franchise Model. https://oxygenhub.org/psaplants/.
- Open O2: Hub for Innovation and Information on Oxygen Concentrators. https://www.openo2.org/home.
- Every Breath Counts Oxygen Plant Fix List. https://docs.google.com/spreadsheets/d/1JiwNxJrJBimYkibu6joPU-TnzMmqE41c2XDjgDipSyw/edit#gid=0.

Innovation

- WHO. 2021. Compendium of Innovative Health Technologies for Low-Resource Settings. https://www.who.int/publications/i/item/9789240032507.
- EdTechHub, mEducation Alliance, Global Innovation Exchange COVID-19 Innovation Hub. https://covid19innovationhub.org/covid-19-recognized-innovations.

Clinical

Essential Medicines and Devices

- WHO. Model Lists of Essential Medicines. https://www.who.int/groups/expert-committee-on-selection-and-use-of-essential-medicines/essential-medicines-lists.
- WHO. 2017. Model List of Essential Medicines (EML).
- WHO. 2017. Model List of Essential Medicines for Children (EMLc).
- WHO. 2015. Interagency Medical Devices for Essential Interventions for Reproductive, Maternal, Newborn, and Child Health. https://apps.who.int/iris/handle/10665/205490.

Clinical Guidelines and Standards

- WHO. 2016. Pocket Book of Hospital Care for Children (2nd edition). 2013. Also available as WHO e-Pocket Book of Hospital Care for Children. https://www.who.int/publications/i/item/978-92-4-154837-3.
- WHO. 2016. Oxygen Therapy for Children: A Manual for Health Workers. https://apps.who.int/iris/handle/10665/204584.
- WHO. 2016. Pediatric Emergency Triage, Assessment and Treatment: Care of Critically-Ill Children: Updated Guidelines. https://apps.who.int/iris/handle/10665/204463.
- WHO. 2018. Standards for Improving the Quality of Care for Children and Young Adolescents in Health Facilities. https://www.who.int/publications/i/item/9789241565554.
- WHO. 2016. Standards for Improving Quality of Maternal and Newborn Care in Health Facilities. https://www.who.int/publications/i/item/9789241511216.

Training

- Open Critical Care Education Hub. https://opencriticalcare.org/.
  - Oxygen and COVID-19 Resource Library.
  - Oxygen Supply and Delivery FAQ.
- COVID-19 Catalog of Training Resources for Health Care Workers Compiled by PATH. https://tableau.path.org/t/COVID-19RespiratoryCare/views/COVID-19CatalogofTrainingResources/ReadMe?:isGuestRedirectFromVizportal=y&:embed=y.
- UNICEF Oxygen Training and Resources Repository. https://bit.ly/OxygenResources.